Dammit, Just Ask!

'Dammit, Just Ask!'

The essential guide on how to get more out of life and business

J. PAUL NADEAU

Contents

DEDICATIONS

To my beloved family, whom I love deeply.

INTRODUCTION

"Believe you can, and you're halfway there."
~ Theodore Roosevelt.

If someone had told me in late 2019 that by mid-March, 2020, most of the globe would be in lockdown under quarantine and that millions and millions of people would be out of work with thousands dying from some deadly virus every day, I would have thought that person crazy. I may have even smiled, shook my head in disbelief and given them a 'Yeah, right…' look, thinking they'd binge watched some apocalypse series on Netflix or Amazon Prime, and simply got spooked and needed to shake off the nightmare. But not only did *that* happen in 2020, so much more craziness has come along; and as I write this, we're only into the month of September, and my gut tells me there's more ugliness coming our way.

> **"Let us never negotiate out of fear. But let us never fear to negotiate".**
> **~ John f. Kennedy**

2020 has so far been a shit-show of unprecedented proportions, and there's no signs of it letting up soon. First there were devastating brush fires that raged across Australia burning some 18.6M hectares of land and killing and/or displacing nearly three *billion* animals, driving some species almost into extinction. That news started our year off and the world grieved for the loss of so many animals and the horror our Australian friends were living. Not too long after that, a deadly virus emerged out of China, it is believed, that we've come to know as COVID-19, and it rapidly spread across the globe, sickening millions and killing thousands upon thousands. It took a while for some world leaders to 'catch on' to the fact that this global pandemic was extremely deadly and was here to stay for a while, so it required being taken seriously or lose out to a virus smaller than a grain of salt that could possible take out half of the worlds' population. Countries locked down, and people lost their jobs, income, security, freedom to move about socially, and more. The economy was paralyzed and the loss to so many, especially the poor, was unimaginable.

Among the many causalities was our sense of hope. The quarantine not only meant that millions across the globe could no longer work, it also meant that we couldn't socialize as we once did; and for many it meant they couldn't visit sick or aging family members, or even attend their loved ones' funerals. Weddings were put off. Single people living alone grew more depressed, and for many who did have folks living with them, being cooped up led to a staggering rise in domestic violence and abuse. The divorce rate would undoubtedly sky rocket, once the courts were back in operation, and people grew angrier and more depressed the longer the pandemic hung in... and it's still hanging in as I write these words. That anxiety and depression, like the plague, is still here and not likely going away anytime soon. A vaccine has not yet been developed and a number of people across the globe think it's all one big hoax, so they defy the social distancing guidelines and laws and help spread the virus even more. But that's our new reality and that's not all 2020 had to deal us.

To add even more to this year of hell, a black man by the name of George Floyd was killed by a racist white cop and it was all caught on video. That brutal, senseless and criminal act of homicide led to the *Black Lives Matter* movement, and it erupted into global protests against the mistreatment of black people by the police with demands to defund and even get rid of the police in places. There's so much more shit I could write here, like killer bees, West Nile disease carrying mosquitos, California wildfires and more, but I'll stop here. It leaves one to wonder if an Alien invasion may be next.

But I'm not here to depress you. I'm simply pointing out our new reality. I believe that we, as one race, have survived all the crap that's come our way so far, and we'll survive this too. So, what does all this doom and gloom have to do with negotiating, you may be asking. A lot, actually. People remain understandably anxious, depressed, uncertain about the future, jobless, and out of hope. COVID-19 has changed our world and how we operate – and negotiate. Many businesses have closed – never to reopen. It's at times like this that you either make it, or you crash and burn. Our landscape has changed and we need to change with it. Perhaps you're one of COVID-19's financial victims: you may have lost your job, your profession, your income and you're hope. But you know what? 'Making it' is a choice. No matter where you may find yourself right now, you can create something new and worthwhile. It may be something altogether new – a transformation that requires reinventing oneself. But you can do it. Knowing how to negotiate and ask for what you want in a new world will help you get there.

Reinventing yourself is a choice and requires work, and in many instances, it requires the help and cooperation of others to get you to where you want to be. We're not in this world alone. We often count on others to get to where we want to be. I know it's not easy for many of us out here. There's an urgent need for many of us to reinvent, rebuild and recover. We have the ability to choose our responses to what's happening, and do something about it. Knowing how to ask and negotiate for what you want and need can help restore that hope some feel they've lost. That, and a great deal more, as you'll soon discover.

Before all this global craziness and loss, it had never ceased to surprise me how so many people just didn't ask for what they wanted in life. To me, asking and negotiating should come as naturally to us as breathing, especially now that life has taken such a horrific downward turn. The skills of asking and negotiating for what you want and need are more important than ever before. Picking ourselves up from here, for many, is going to be hard and scary. Without the right tools, rebuilding anything is next to impossible. Having the right tools is imperative, and the art of negotiating in life and in business is one of those essential rebuilding tools. So why is it that so many people are not asking for what they want and need, especially now?

The way I see it, the reasons so many people **don't ask** and **don't get** simply comes down to one of three **F**'s:
1. **Fear** (afraid of being told '*No*')
2. **Forgetfulness** (not *thinking* to ask in the first place) and;
3. **Familiarity** (not knowing *how* to ask).

> Let's cover these topics and more in depth, so that your opportunities for renewed security and income – and much more – can begin now, shall we? This is about getting you to where you deserve to be. Let me start by saying this: it doesn't have to be that difficult of a life for those who struggle, especially when one knows how to work each of the 3 **F's** keeping them from asking, negotiating and getting more of what they want and need - in every area of their lives.

A good book on negotiations is as much a book on effective communication, and communicating well is an essential element to any successful interaction in life. Negotiating is a language of rapport building and deploying excellent interpersonal relationships, and that's what you're about to discover in the pages of this book. I know some of you might be overwhelmed and uncertain right now. God knows I've experienced those emotions. But when life throws us a curve ball or hits us square between the eyes, we must pick ourselves up, dust ourselves off and look it right in the eyes and shout, "Batter up!" with all the determination to succeed as we can muster. We can't wait to be saved or we'll simply drown in our own sadness, desperation and hopelessness. We've gotta take control of our lives, and by picking up this book, that's exactly what you're doing. This book is for you and your wellbeing, and I'm going to share what I know with you so that you'll have some of the best rebuilding tools available to start your new life 'beyond this COVID Craziness!'

****

Now, as much as there are several excellent books on the market out there on the topic of negotiating, what makes this one different than most is that this book is a book on *asking* **and** *negotiating* for what you want, in this new COVID world, and it has been written for the day-to-day negotiator as well as the business negotiator - by someone who knows how to negotiate, even the toughest of negotiations – a former hostage negotiator. I'll keep this material as simple as possible for you so that it will be easy to understand and easy to apply. But there's more. Face-to-face negotiating is going to be rarer now due to COVID-19, and with the new safety measures and adjustments that have all been put in place, it only makes sense that we adapt accordingly. We're going to have to adjust to this new world, which means that for the time being, much of our business negotiating, and some of our life negotiations, will be done via email or video in the many platforms now available (Zoom, Skype etc…). Are there pitfalls to this? You betcha there are, so understanding how to navigate them will help in your recovery and successes.

For instance, negotiating by email has pitfalls too many negotiators ignore or simply don't understand. Research shows that negotiators experience less satisfaction with email negotiating. They experience less rapport and less future trust in their partners. Why? For example, with email negotiating:

- There may be a greater tendency to lie, exaggerate, bluff or intimidate

- Negotiators don't feel the pressure of having to prepare for a "live performance," and consequently, often prepare less.

- Because it's more difficult to build rapport and trust through email, there's often less focus on mutual interests, and more on self-serving positions and demands.

- Communication challenges can arise easily, which may include rudeness, ambiguous messages, misinterpretations, and ill-conceived reactions. Rapport is not possible when that takes place.

- It's easier to say "no" in an email, and brainstorming with your team on how to handle objections is not always possible. Intimidation can get the best of the negotiator and fear might just get the best of the negotiator.

Because of these downsides, email negotiations can inhibit the trust and mutual understanding that builds and sustains rapport, so conflicts or misunderstandings can easily degenerate or worsen. But I'll cover how to recognize and avoid these pitfalls later in this book. You can negotiate like a pro despite these current roadblocks. It simply requires understanding how.

I'm a story teller, so you can expect a few of my personal and professional stories to seep into this material as you read on. In each story you'll find something you can use in your world of negotiations, guaranteed. As you read them, imagine how they may apply to your personal and/or professional circumstances. Don't just read the stories for their entertainment value – and I assure you, some will be quite entertaining indeed. Instead, pause, think and imagine if what I was going through, and what I did and *how* I did it, could help *you* positively influence the outcome of your negotiations and circumstances. That's how you'll get more from what you read. I'll start with a personal story, taking you to a time in the 1970s. Oh how I'd like to revisit the 70's knowing what I know today.

The year was 1974, and I was 18. I may have looked like your typical 18-year-old 70's kid, right out of a television sitcom, with long hair down to my shoulders, still wearing my psychedelic shirts from the 60s, but I didn't consider myself a *typical* teen. Not at all. I'd earned a brass set of cojones the hard way by then, long before turning 16, which, when I look back at it, have served me well. I had a jerk of an alcoholic and abusive father, who, not out of the goodness-of-his-stone crusted heart, taught me some pretty valuable lessons on how to get what I wanted out of life that I managed to carry with me on job hunts and other life matters as a teenager, and throughout my life to this very day.

Turns out his abuse and control of me backfired, and instead of breaking my spirit, it prepped me to become a badass negotiating warrior. He indirectly taught me how to get more of what I wanted and needed by teaching me to have the guts to go for what I wanted. No school - other than the school of hard knocks I'd been born into, could have blessed or prepared me any better for what was to come than the lessons taught to me by my old man, the devils' spawn. Lessons I otherwise may never have discovered had it not been for the way he treated me and my family. Bad stuff happens, but sometimes that stuff happens for a reason that we don't always see at the time. You just can't let the bad shit define your life.

That year, immediately after graduating from high school, I enrolled in a law enforcement course at a Toronto, Ontario community college, and I wanted a part-time job that would be, in some way, in line with my vision of becoming a cop. I'd dreamed of being a detective since I was 7 because I wanted to arrest my old man for what he put our family through. I don't quite know how I came across this brilliant idea, but I did. The thought occurred to me to apply for the position of an undercover store detective in a major department store to apprehend shoplifters. 'Why not?', I figured.

Perhaps today that doesn't seem like such a big deal, but in 1974, I could think of no one my age who was a store detective. We lived in a different era back then, and many of today's young people, some of you reading this included, have greater life-experience than some of us back then because of the fact you've been exposed to so much more than many of us were back in that era. The world has evolved so rapidly, providing you with so much more experience, good and bad, and, happily, as you'll discover: opportunity. It may not seem like that now due to COVID, but opportunity is there. You just got to look for it, hunt it down like a warrior and cease it. I'll get into that later.

So, at 18, I wanted a job that may have seemed ridiculous to everyone but me in 1974, but I decided I was going to go for it anyway. "What's the worst that could happen?" I thought. Well, dah, they could say 'No' - but is that something that should hold me back from asking? Heck no, I concluded. It's what I wanted, and I figured, "Why not give it your best shot, Nadeau? Why not *just ask* already?" So, there I was: a longed haired 70s kid standing in front of a major department store about ready to ask for a job as a store detective at the age of 18. In I went and asked to speak directly to the security manager. Odd and bewildered looks I got in droves, along with the question, "May I ask what this is about?" "I'd rather speak to the security manager directly, if I may," was my reply. I was told to wait. Ten minutes later, a distinguished, bewildered, well-dressed man sporting a handsome beard appeared and identified himself as Chet Jackson, the security manager.

I asked if I might speak with him privately. He led me to his office and had me take a chair. Since I'd managed to get through the door, it was time for me to unleash the courage my folks had taught me (yeah, my mom was a great example of courage, having put up with the beast for so many years) and just get on with it. I'd used it before, many times since the age of 14 in my first bus-boy job, so it wasn't anything new. I immediately launched into my proposal at an alarming rapid-fire pace, much like the sound of a machine gun firing off relentlessly: "I'd like to work for you as an undercover store detective! My goal is to become a policeman when I turn twenty-one, and I've enrolled in a community college taking a law enforcement course. Now, I know I'm young, but who would ever suspect someone as young as me with long hair catching shoplifters?! Nobody! I'd do a good job for you, Mr. Jackson. You have my word!"

I must have struck a nerve, because a smile came to his face and he leaned comfortably back in his chair, and I, well, I scrambled to catch my breath, happy I didn't chicken out. I had done it. I had just asked. The worst was over and he didn't laugh me out of his office or call on his security personnel to haul my ass out the door.

We spent the next forty-five minutes in pleasant, relaxed conversation, and at one point, Mr. Jackson excused himself and left the office for a few minutes. He returned accompanied by the general manager of the store. I was introduced to him, shook his hand, smiled, and spent no more than five minutes passing the breeze with him, after which he excused himself and called Chet to the side. Chet then returned with an announcement: "We don't have any security jobs available at the moment, and our security staff are, well, much older than you, Paul. But... we're making an exception in your case. You're hired. You start next week!"

Yeah, I had a vision of getting what I'd asked for, but I wasn't expecting to get it *that very day*. I started the very next week.

I worked there until I became a cop at the age of twenty-one, and loved every minute of it... except for that *one* arrest which resulted in torn knee ligaments, major reconstructive surgery and a plaster cast I was stuck wearing for three months, complete with harness, not to mention the long and painful physiotherapy that followed. That period I didn't enjoy so much. The rest was a tremendous blast that I would never have had if I hadn't just asked.

***

Finding the courage to go for what you
want, despite your fears, is one of the first
steps to getting what you want out of life.

***

Why a 70s throwback story of a long-haired teenager asking for a job to start off a book on asking and negotiating, you may be asking? Because, even in the simplest of stories, you, dear reader, can see the value and importance of a few of the many lessons you're about to be introduced to by reading on. For instance, in the story I just told you, here are the key points – your take-aways:

- Go after what you want in life, no matter how big or ridiculous it may sound to others;

- Take risks and just do it, because NOT taking risks and going after what you want will guarantee you that you'll be exactly where you are at the same time next year, and the year after that…
- Ask for what you want, despite your fears. That's what helps *get* you what you want. If you don't ask, you just won't get.

Is it as simple as 'just asking'? Not quite, otherwise there would be no need for this book. There's a method, and it's really quite simple.

Ground rules to make it happen

Let me first get into what this book is, and what it's not. These are the simple ground rules needed to help make it all happen for you. Consider this book an instructional manual complete with guideposts, principles and formulae, used regularly and successfully in a host of negotiations. In my case, I used them successfully in hostage and crisis negotiations, criminal interrogations and in my every-day life and business negotiations; in your case, they'll be used in your day-to-day personal life and/or business negotiations. All of what you're about to discover here will be easily translatable and will apply to your personal and professional matters, most assuredly.

What this book aims to do for you, is to help you develop your *influence 'savvy'* through exploratory dialogue and a host of other easy to use techniques. The art and science of successful negotiations is one based upon firmly establishing rapport with your negotiatee[1] as a segue to building relationships of mutual trust, respect and likeability - absolutely essential to *every* worthwhile, productive and successful negotiation – be it personal or

---

[1] To simplify who I mean by the term negotiatee, consider them family members, friends, co-workers, professional business people and anyone you'll be asking something from or negotiating with.

professional. Dig through whatever good book you come by on negotiating and if they don't encourage relationship building, toss them out. They suck and they're useless. A trustworthy relationship is what you're after, because people will be happy to deal with those they know, like and trust, and that's possible only by establishing a positive, solid relationship.

There are guideposts to follow to accomplish this. They're not hard to follow, and they'll help you get what you want.

Guidepost number one: No manipulating or coercion, whatsoever

This ought to be obvious to most, but some knuckleheads out there just don't get it. One of the things that led to my many successes as a cop and peacekeeper is the way I treated those I dealt with, no matter who they were or what they'd done. I wasn't out to lie, cheat, coerce or manipulate anyone. My job as a cop was to get them to comply and cooperate willingly, whether that was acquiring a statement from a reluctant witness, a confession from a killer, or the release of hostages being held at gunpoint. Using an approach that builds trust and likeability is what works. With that said, I think you know where I'm coming from and where I want you to be: this book does not support manipulating your negotiatee in any ill-intended way, shape or form, and so I happily introduce to you my first guidepost: no manipulating, whatsoever. You won't have to.

The lessons you're about to discover are not meant to be used to take advantage of, or manipulate, or intimidate anyone to get what you want. My PIER™© Negotiating method of positive influence won't teach you how to negotiate solely for what you're after at whatever unholy cost. I don't believe in that kind of negotiating, because it always comes at a cost, and it's simply unethical and wrong.

Once you use the principles' I'm about to introduce you to, the guideposts within the pages of this book will help you to build mutually-beneficial relationships which may last well beyond your initial negotiation for ages to come – which, in turn, translates to the possibility of any number of other amazing and possible benefits which arise from these mutually-beneficial relationships. Being aware of the differences between manipulation and friendly, effective persuasion is an absolute must.

Simply put, the techniques I present to you in this book are scientific and psychological – and they work without resorting to underhanded manipulation. I want you to become a badass negotiator, not a bad ass.

"Manipulative people do not understand the concept of boundaries. They are relentless in their pursuit of what they want, and they have no regard for who gets hurt along the way." – Author unknown.

The wisdom of a philosophical fighter

Bruce Lee, a remarkable philosopher and human being on so many levels, once said that 'life itself is your teacher, and you're in a state of constant learning.' I can certainly attest to that - at least it has been my experience. But life is only your teacher when you *choose* to be its student.

To expand further on how life itself has been one of my greatest teachers, I'd discovered quite by circumstance how to ask and negotiate for what I wanted at an early age, albeit, on a rather novice scale, but I was never, ever without a job. This should be of particular interest to you if you're at a stage in your life where you're not getting nearly enough of what you want and deserve in life. And for anyone whose lost their jobs or income because of

COVID19, I'm talking to you. Negotiating just one deal or consideration will more than pay for the cost of this book, and that will be just the beginning. God knows that in these COVID-19 times, we need every tool we can get our hands on to succeed.

I hope you're already imagining the possibilities of how knowing how to negotiate and ask for what you want in life will improve almost every aspect of your private and professional life. Knowing how to ask and negotiate does not simply translate into financial benefits either, as great as they will be. Along with getting more breaks, benefits and deals, you'll also develop a self-confidence that will take you to more places than you ever imagined possible for yourself, simply by knowing how to ask for it.

For me, even as a kid, knowing the basics got me so much more than my school buddies and people much older than myself got back then. I bought my first car the day I turned 16, had money in the bank, and had a self-assuredness not too many of my 16-year-old friends had back then, or any other 16-year-olds I knew of in the '70s. I came by most of my courage and negotiation skills due to my father's demands and unreasonable expectations, and by watching him when he wasn't behaving like Mr. Hyde, Dr. Jekyll's evil persona.

My salesmanship savvy I credit primarily to my beloved mother. Both had taught me how to be courageous, for damn sure. My mom taught me how to stand up to my fears even when the devil himself was standing before me, daring me not to take another damn step forward. Both my folks taught me to grow a pair, stand up to my whatever came my way and knock down doors. It has served me well, and if you're on board and want to know how YOU CAN get the most out of *your* life, what you're about to be introduced to *will* change your life.

But first, you must choose to go from 'wanting more out of life' to 'getting more out of life,' and that takes commitment and action. It's not hard to do. Don't just WANT: WANT, DO and then GET.

***

Wanting and courage just aren't enough.
To get what you're after, you must follow
both these with the correct action.

***

I might as well warn you now – I have a habit of thinking big and going after what I want. I'm not unrealistic, nor should you be; but I do aim high. That's something I suggest you start doing. When you think small, you get small. Think big, get big. That's the way it works. How that applies to asking and negotiating will become apparent very soon.

The problem with a ton of people is that they dream too small and settle accordingly; or they don't dream at all. This makes me sad for them. Some never give a thought on how they can change their unsatisfying circumstances because they've adapted to their misery. That's called 'learned helplessness'. They cry themselves to sleep, walk around stressed all the time, turn to booze or drugs to dull the pain of their sad lives, and give in. They settle for minimum wage jobs they hate, barely have enough money to pay the rent at the end of the month and spend more lonely nights they care to admit watching the tube; simply because they didn't think to ask or have the courage or know-how to go after what they wanted. They're often far too afraid of moving beyond their comfort zones. And with the reality of COVId-19 settling in, dependence on alcohol and drugs has skyrocketed and people are losing hope. Does that sound like anyone *you* might know?

My goal is to help you dream big and ask big, despite this COVID Craziness, with the confidence that you'll now get much more out of life, once you master the PIER™ principles of asking and negotiating, no matter what your current circumstances may be, or what you've lost. I also intend to help some of you who may have been the victims of authority let-down. What do I mean by this? Parenting and school practices that left you confused about how to go about getting what you want out of life because you were not taught how to, through no fault of your own. For many of you reading this now, you were told you were ever-so-special, and could get *anything* you wanted in life – but, dammit, you were never told *how* to go about getting it, and whatever assurances you got were painfully unrealistic. Just look at where we are today. Who could have predicted this shit? And has any of those promises withstood the reality of time and what life dealt you?

I'm thinking 'not' for many of you.

You suffered because the education system didn't demand you to work for rewards, nor did some of your folks. Some of you were handed rewards for simply showing up, and you did not taste the sweat and pain it takes to compete and get what you're after. Now you're understandably confused, disillusioned, and angry, and this book will give you the answers you're after when it comes to going for what you want. You bet your ass you deserve it too.

Understanding that it is your right to ask for what you want in life is a perfect start. Discovering how to ask and how to negotiate for what you want is the next step in getting what you want in life.

Involuntary blindness and the loss of childhood innocence

I started this book off by expressing how surprised I was that so few people either don't know how to ask for what they want, or they don't think to. Perhaps one of the reasons for not asking and negotiating is because you've lost your childhood, in-grained fearless nerve to ask for what you want; or maybe you're simply afraid of being told 'no.' As I mentioned earlier, it could also be that you're not sure *how* to ask; or it might possibly come down to something as simple as you just don't 'think' to ask – we are often blind to the very opportunities that stare us right in the face.

Whatever your reasons for not asking and/or negotiating, the consequence of not doing so is that it sadly leaves those of you who don't falling short of getting what you want and deserve. And by not asking for what you want and deserve (stay with me here), you may be depriving someone else from getting what they want and deserve in life too. Yes, you read that right. You may very well be the reason someone else doesn't get what they wanted and needed because you never asked or negotiated with them for what *you* wanted.

Confused? Think about it: Consider for a moment that you might be the ideal employee for a company you're interested in working for, or the ideal tenant, or the ideal partner for someone you've admired from a distance: but you chickened out and never asked for a shot at the title in the first place, or you just didn't know how. Who loses? You all lose.

I, for one, would much rather get more out of this life, even at the risk of being told 'no', wouldn't you?! You've got a damn good chance they're going to say 'yes' more often than they're going to say 'no', especially once you develop the skills of a hostage negotiator. And another thing: 'No' isn't necessarily the end. As you'll discover by reading on, it's often simply the wonderful beginning.

Understanding that it's your right to ask for what you want in life is a great start. Discovering the 'how, when, and why' of asking and negotiating for what you want are the next steps in getting what you want from life. Knowing how to ask and negotiate is like being given the keys to a dream sports car and a precise map (or these days, an up-to-date navigation system) to whichever destination you choose.

Both will help you navigate through what first appears to be a complex series of highways and roadblocks, which, once strategically traveled, will take you right to where you planned to be. The more you travel that road, the more familiar it will become, and soon you'll be navigating it and many others, effortlessly. Going after what you want and deserve will become second nature: as though you were on constant auto-pilot. You picked up your keys when you invested in this book. Are you ready to ride?

***

You may be the very answer to someone else's needs, wants and desires. All you have to do to find out, is to ask.

***

PART 1

TO GET WHAT *YOU* WANT; YOU MUST GIVE THEM SOME OF WHAT THEY WANT.

Chapter One

IT CAN'T BE ALL ABOUT YOU

Getting what you want is an **exchange**, no matter how small or big that exchange may be, and it must always work to the advantage of each of the parties involved. Negotiating and asking for what you want should never be about getting the upper hand on someone or making it all about you. That's a dumbass way of getting what you want – a bully's way - and you're sure to regret it. In fact, doing so is like building a house of cards - it *will* come tumbling down eventually, along with those objectives you had, with perhaps irreparable consequences. The only question is, when?

It may also cause you some substantial reputation damage, and once your reputation is damaged, you may never recover from it. You're better than that, and what's more, if you're reading this, you *do* want more out of life, so understand now that you just can't make it all about you. To get what you want, you must give them something *they* want.

***

Getting what you want is an exchange. We
give to get, even if what we give is simply a
feeling of trust at first.

***

My warriors' stripes and what they mean to you

As a former hostage negotiator, criminal interrogator and international peacekeeper, I've discovered a great deal on how to positively influence behavior and reach mutually beneficial agreements with my clients[2]. I've evolved significantly since that job negotiation with Chet, the store security manager I told you of earlier, and it's paid off remarkably well.

My expertise and success do not solely come from a number of in-depth courses taught on negotiations and interrogation by some of the very best experts in these fields. No, I've got something more. My expertise also comes from having dealt with hundreds of tough and often heart-wrenching cases involving criminals, victims, witnesses, hostage takers, suicidal and desperate individuals, and more. It comes from having applied the techniques I'd been taught to each case to bring about the most successful of outcomes imaginable, often under duress. It grew by learning **and** by doing. I experienced the blood, sweat and tears that came from immersing myself totally into a craft I wanted to master, no matter what obstacles or challenges came my way.

I became a skilled and proficient asker *and* negotiator by using and modifying the tools I'd been taught to make them my own. I developed a few techniques of my own along the way that have proven to work exceptionally well. This evolved expertise and know-how is what qualifies me to be your guide, and I have a negotiators flashlight to help you find *your* way. I earned my stripes, and now it's time you earned yours.

---

[2] My clients were those I negotiated with and asked consideration from: victims, witnesses, suspects, criminals, hostage takers and so forth. They became my 'negotiatee's', a term I'll explain shortly and will be using throughout this book.

Repetition equals mastery

"Repetition is the mother of learning, the father of action, which makes it the architect of accomplishment." Zig Ziglar.

As a former police instructor both in Canada and in the Middle East, I'm warning ya' all upfront that you may find I repeat myself on key points more than once; but I do so deliberately. I got in the habit of repeating key concepts in my many diverse global classes over the years, to help my students remember what I intended them to remember (and for what might be on the test), and I'll do the same for you here. The more you hear it, the more it will stick, like eggs to a non-coated frying pan. No, there won't be a test once you're done reading this book - at least not one given by me. Your test(s) will be to apply what you've discovered here whenever you can; in asking and negotiating for what you want from this very point on. I want you all to become superstar, badass negotiators! My wish for you is that you commit to memory as much of this material as possible, anchoring the principles, guideposts and acronym I'll be sharing with you to memory. The more you hear them, the more they'll stick. The more they'll stick to your frying pan, the better it is for you. You will, after all, be negotiators and skillful askers by the end of this book.

What is a negotiation, anyway?

It seems only logical to examine what a negotiation actually is before getting into the methods on how to do it, doesn't it? I think so, so here's my definition: Negotiations are, in their simplest forms, exchanges between two or more people for the purpose of reaching agreements, be it in life or in business. They're discussions with purpose, and that purpose is to reach agreements or understandings that satisfy the mutual interests of all parties, individuals or groups of people involved. It's that simple, and I intend to keep it that simple.

One of the very first things to keep in mind when your goal is to positively influence the behavior or actions of others through negotiation is to try to see things through the others' eyes – seek to see and understand their point of view as you work together at reaching mutually beneficial agreements. Successful negotiations are very much about making successful connections, and seeking to first understand them is an excellent way of truly connecting. It's amazing what may happen when you connect with another human being that may help you reach your objective.

What's in this for you?

'Life and business' interactions account for all your dealings and negotiations with those around you: from the people who matter the most to you, to those you've just met. They additionally account for those opportunities you come by or create on your own to help you improve your current position in life and business. Since our world turned upside-down because of the coronavirus, it's more important than ever to create our own opportunities and go for what we want.

That could be something as simple as negotiating for a break on rent, even now (I'll provide an example of how doing so once saved me $6,000.00 a year using the principles of PIER™ Negotiating later in this book); or it may be negotiating a better price for a car, or asking for a much-needed job. It may involve negotiating with your kids to get them to do their chores; negotiating with your spouse, partner, or friends. It may also involve negotiating a huge business contract or the terms of a legal contract of some kind. The sky is the limit – you're only limited by what you *cannot* imagine for yourself.

Who will benefit from asking and negotiating like a hostage negotiator?

Simple. You will, that's who. This book is intended for everyone who wants to get more out of life **and** in business. It's for those who want to ask fearlessly for what they want, and with the confidence that they'll have a much greater chance of getting what they ask for by using the principles and guideposts offered here. It's for the student, worker, parent, husband, wife, teacher and everyone else in-between. Do you see yourself in there? I sure hope so, because you matter, and I wrote this book for you.

I won't neglect the business professional (I haven't omitted you from this work). The principles I offer here will also help you seal more deals, so I welcome you to join us on this journey. In fact, if you are a business professional who negotiates for a living, you'll find blocks of information specific - but not restricted - to business; that which I'll call "Business Bulletin(s)."

*For the non-business, everyday life negotiator, I encourage you to read these business bulletins as well. You'll not only find the material informative, but you'll also discover how to easily transfer much, if not all of what you read in those bulletins, to *your* day-to-day life negotiations. This is a book on professional asking *and* negotiating, for the day-to-day **and** professional asker and negotiator, so all of what you read here will at some time, and in some way, apply to *your* given circumstances, guaranteed. They will benefit everyone who reads them.

Life is a bunch of business negotiations: make 'em all count

Have you, the day-to-day negotiator, ever considered that your life is full of 'business' negotiation opportunities? Think about it. You engage in business with others when you negotiate in your day-to-day dealings - almost, *if not*, every day of your life. The 'business of life' is all around you.

When I say *business*, consider how this applies to you. Is it, for you, asking to meet with someone to negotiate an agreement or understanding in an important personal matter? Or might it be negotiating for a better position at work? Is it, for you, asking to be considered for a special position in an organization you're a member of, or negotiating a better interest rate at the bank? You decide. I'll provide many more examples of how this applies to everyone along the way so that you will easily see how incredible vast this can get. By doing that, you'll understand how much this applies to your everyday life negotiations and you'll look for more opportunities to turn this around for yourself using your new talents.

We're damn near limitless

We're damn near limitless. The way I see it, the only limitations we have are those we place on ourselves. The only obstacles keeping us from moving forward and enjoying the life we deserve to live are the ones we choose not to eradicate and move beyond. These 'captors' are the chains of hopelessness, defeat and/or sadness we knowingly or unconsciously wrap ourselves in, making certain we secure the shackles we've forged with our imaginary padlocks; or the cages of solitude, inaction, and self-doubt we unconsciously make our home: each a sad creation of *our* own doing. All of these will prevent us from getting what we want if we let them.

The incredible and liberating reality is that it is *we* who are in control of our destinies, our lives, our successes *and* our choices. We can choose to be limitless, action oriented, confident and determined; or we can choose to remain imprisoned in our self-created dungeons. The fact is that if it is we who have 'hostaged' ourselves, then we can just as easily *un-hostage* ourselves, provided we understand how. We can't afford to leave our rescue or successes in the hands of any other person, thing or misdirected hope – whatever that may be. Otherwise, we may find ourselves sitting on a "rock" of our own solitude, growing old awaiting some perhaps nameless, faceless rescue party to free us from the unhappy circumstances we find ourselves in.

Once we realize that the wilderness of unhappiness, we find ourselves in is a landscape of our own making—one created by our own minds—we can then act to get out of the uncomfortable place in which we have somehow landed[3]. This applies to unlocking the chains of fear and self-doubt that are holding us back from asking and getting what we want in life. The rescue I speak of can only come from within.

By accepting self-sabotaging and limiting behaviors, we become hostages to ourselves, and we hostage the limitless power and opportunities that are ours for the taking - that which we rightfully deserve.

No one holds the key to our rescue, potential, happiness or success, but us. I discovered this impetus once I had finally rescued *myself* from the rock of solitude I'd found myself on. For me, that miraculously and curiously happened in grade seven. That discovery eventually led me to believe that since I could rescue myself and create my own destinies, I must certainly possess the ability to get more out of life. I was quite young to have discovered this invaluable life lesson and the many discoveries I've made since have enriched my life in ways

---

[3] From "Take Control of Your Life", J. Paul Nadeau ©2018, HarperCollins Canada
Take Control of Your Life

I once could never have imagined. Eventually, I went from 'crawling' to ask, to running to ask.

Something else occurred to me. Not right away, but over time. When looking back at all I'd been through, it occurred to me that I had a choice on how to look at, and feel about, what I'd experienced – especially the bad stuff.

The passing of time and my new outlook on my unlimited power clarified that for me. One point of view would keep me reflecting sadly on my past misadventures, adversities and setbacks, hostaging me from getting more out of life, whereas the other would have me marvel at how things turned out *because* of what I'd been through and what meaning I'd 'chosen' to attach to what I'd been through. I chose the latter: to look at most of the adversities and setbacks I'd suffered as not something that happened "to" me, but rather as something that happened "for" me. That thinking gifted me with a new perspective, awareness and welcomed understanding. It should do the very same for you, too.

How you choose to see your adversities will directly affect your behavior and your outcomes. How you choose to approach your negotiatees' will have just as much of an effect. Are you there to do something "to" them or something "for" them? Answering this question and behaving accordingly will influence the outcome, whichever way you choose it to.

As you reflect on your own life, ask yourself: are there adversities from your past that have happened *to you* that beg to be re-examined to discover how they've actually happened *for you*? Could those adversities and setbacks be holding you back from going after what you want? I bet there are. These may be the very roadblocks that have prevented you from moving confidently forward in getting what you want and deserve in life. Stop reading, and take a few minutes to examine them. See how attaching a different, more empowering meaning to them, whenever possible, may immediately improve the quality of your life and set you free to move forward. It will be liberating. It's been so for me. You may be thinking, 'Dude, really?' Yeah, really. Try it. Dwelling on the past, especially on missed opportunities or on past hardships will undoubtedly affect your current state of mind. And you'll want a strong state of mind to get the best in life.

***

Sometimes things don't happen to you –
they happen for you.
***

When I began to look for the positive outcomes that evolved from the adversities I'd suffered and how they shaped and influenced who I am now, I found the strength, understanding and focus I needed to move forward with new found determination. Success and rewards followed. For example, I never would have become a cop, saved lives and helped so many people had I not been abused as a child by my father. I would never have promised myself at the tender age of seven that when I grew up, I'd become a cop and arrest people like my father. I had un-hostaged myself from the cages of my own creation, the dungeons of my past, and with that new-found freedom, vision and relief, I set out to get more out of life. This discovery eventually led to negotiating, asking and going after what I wanted in every area of my life. It will do the same for you.

Again, what does this all have to do with asking and negotiating for what you want in life, you may be asking?

'Un-hostaging' yourself is the first step in your journey to successful negotiations

You can't move forward if you're locked in a cage, even if it's one of your own creation. If you're a hostage to yourself, un-hostaging yourself is the very first step in getting the most out of life. Doing so sets you free and helps align you perfectly to go for what you want by providing you with the strength and freedom to do so, and that's accomplished by liberating yourself from your past.

Awareness, skill, and determination are the next things to discover and develop. We were never meant to be under the control of nagging voices of self-loathing or doubt in our heads that tell us we're not good enough or that we're not worthy enough of getting whatever we want in life. Hell, no. We were - and are - meant for so much more than a self-manufactured state of limitations, hopelessness, and self-sabotage.

That's why discovering that we become hostages to our pasts and our very own self-imposed limitations by *choice* is so awesomely liberating. It provides us with a gift of awareness, which is the first step to working our way to ultimate freedom, action and then on to success and happiness. The only one stopping us from doing all of this, is us; that, and know-how – which you're about to get in spades.

When you un-hostage yourself from your past, more specifically: when you free yourself from self-sabotaging beliefs, you align yourself to become that much more than you once were. When you develop vision without borders by liberating yourself and work at building the confidence and determination it takes to go for what you want in life and in business, you become unstoppable. To do so is to become limitless, by my definition.

I understand that many of you reading this may not be suffering from self-doubt or self-sabotage, but if you're one of the many who do, even to the *slightest* degree (and that applies to most of us at some point in our lives), then self-doubt *even to the slighest degree* may very well prevent you from getting that deal, that date or that job. Sel-doubt is a dream killer. A killer of deals. A pest that needs to be smacked upside the head, and you're going to discover how to do exactly that.

There is a way you can free yourself to move effortlessly and confidently forward in getting what you want and deserve in life. For those suffering from self-doubt, a new set of liberating beliefs must replace the old, immobilizing ones. This applies to all who feel hostaged at any time in their lives.

Not only must you develop and master these new beliefs and attitudes - but you must also unleash them with Jedi determination through your actions: in your body language, your smile, your eye contact with others and by the very words you use. Sometimes the most difficult person to negotiate with is yourself. Once you've successfully negotiated with yourself, your energy re-emerges and your potential hightens. Doing that makes it easier to negotiate with anyone from that point on.

What you give to others you'll most often get right back. Give them something good.

Smack someone in the face and you'll likely get smacked right back. Flash someone a smile, and your chances are excellent that you'll get one in return. I believe in the theory of reciprocation – in fact, I so believe in it that I advocate it at each of my keynotes, and it's been my personal experience, time and time again, that what you give, you get.

With that principle in mind, I'd walk into an interrogation room and extend my hand to whatever criminal I was about to interview. You'd be amazed how many murderers, gang members, theives and other assortments of criminals would return what they were given. Maybe not at first, but I didn't let up. Eventually, human nature kicked in and they repricated. When I treated them with dignity and respect, they almost always did the same. I'd guestimate it was at least 90% of the time. If they didn't, I'd gently call them on it. I'll get into this in much more depth later, but for now I want to point out that the way in which you approach *your* negotiatee and what you do from that moment on will greatly affect what you'll get in return. How you treat them is how they will almost always treat you back. Simple, isn't it? It's human nature. We are all social people and we need connection and trust to survive.

It's so vitally important, therefor, that you be conscious of the attitude and the energy you project to your negotiatees or anyone you engage with, for that matter, especially when you hope to influence the outcomes of those engagements. Everyone recognizes positive energy and rewards those who send it out in kind. We've all heard of the law of attraction. It applies here. Damn, it applies just about everywhere. You get back what you send out. In negotiating and asking for what you want, that translates to more 'yeses.'

Why talking to yourself can be so wonderfully empowering

What you say to yourself is obviously going to affect your state of mind. It will affect how you feel, and what you'll do, just as much as what you say to others will do the same to them. So, if you're going to talk to yourself, make it positive and upbeat - and tell yourself the *right* things.

13

"Most of us are totally unaware that our inner conversations are the causes of the circumstances of our life." Neville

Once you choose certainty over uncertainty, empowering monologues over a disempowering one, and determination over weakness, you hold the limitless ability to create the most positive *outcomes* for yourself – and that has the magic of attracting the very best life has to offer to you. Your negotiatees will reciprocate when *you* create the desire within them to do so. Give them something they want, give them a good feeling about you and what you have to offer and they'll do the very same for you.

With the right energy, skill, state of mind and attitude, you become a magnet. Those around you will feel the positive energy you transmit, and they'll be naturally and effortlessly drawn to you. They'll be open to giving you what you ask for, or at the very least, on working with you to reach something you'll both be mutually happy with, because they'll feel an immediate connection and attraction to you - and *want to*. That's also known as having charisma.

But to draw the very best of this magnetic charm and charisma out, you'll need to know 'how' to ask for what you want, in addition to the 'why' and 'when.' Using a 'jack-in-the-box' approach to asking and/or negotiating, popping some request or demand at whim without following a plan, expecting your wishes to be granted will not get you far. Even if you are charming. It's foolish thinking and unrealistic. You're not a genie, and there is no magic formula here – or anywhere else for that matter. It's not enough to have the right vibrations and appeal. That's only part of the recipe.

***

Being charming is great and all, but it's not enough. To influence behavior change and get them agreeing with you, you'll have to give them something they're looking for. That could be as simple as giving them a feeling they can trust you.

***

Additionally, a solid foundation must first be built on which to stand, allowing you to move forward, solidly to the next phase. That foundation could be as easy to create as giving them a sense that you can be trusted and may have something they're looking for. Trust is essential – it is the bond that cements us together, no matter what. Without it there is nothing.

The relationship between an emotionally intelligent negotiator and their counterpart essentially duplicates that of a psychotherapist and his patient. The psychotherapist pokes and prods to understand his patient's problems, then turns the responses back onto his patient to get his patient to go in deeper and ultimately change behavior. And that's what great negotiators do.

Getting to this level of emotional intelligence demands opening up your senses, talking less and listening more. You can learn everything you need and a lot more than people are willing to tell you by *watching and listening*. Keep your eyes open and peeled and keep your mouth shut until it's time to open it.

Having the right energy is only one of the essential steps. Looks and charm get you only so far, as they say.

Knowing *how*, *when* and *why* to ask and negotiate are the next fundamental steps to reaching agreements. They provide you with the necessities to ask and negotiate confidently and with skill, providing you the best chance of getting what you're after.

Before we get too far ahead, let me share this with you: before *ever* embarking on negotiating and asking *anyone* for what you want, you'll need to know how to negotiate confidently with *yourself* first. Only then will you be ready to negotiate successfully with others.

The very first person you must positively influence in any negotiation, is you

What do I mean by 'negotiate confidently with yourself first?' As earlier noted, negotiations are, in their simplest form, quests for agreements. They involve a multitude of important principles and guideposts that must be followed precisely to succeed. When *self-*negotiating, your focus and intent will be to reach agreements of value with your 'self' first, followed by the associated action required to bring that negotiation forward. "Okay…what the hell do you mean, Nadeau?" you're likely asking. Good question and I'm glad you're asking. Let me put it this way…

Your primary *internal* conversations and discussions must prepare you for the secondary ones you'll have with others later. I'll explain this concept more clearly in a moment, but first, you must want what it is you're after bad enough to motivate and negotiate *yourself* into taking whatever action it requires to go after it. Simply put, you'll engage in a monologue of positive self-chatter with yourself first, outlining the benefits of moving forward with your goals.

***

If you want something bad enough, you'll
do whatever it takes to get it. If you're
simply in love with the idea of getting it,
your chances of getting it drop to zero.

***

Some of you may be asking right now, "What do you mean I must want it bad enough?!" Well, do you want it bad enough to put effort into planning and executing your ask or negotiation following a proven method of success? Or are you just 'in love' with the idea and *hope* to get whatever it is you're after?

What level of 'going after it' commitment are you ready to use as you develop the skills you require to get what you're after? It's not difficult to do, but you've gotta want it that bad enough to learn how to negotiate and ask for what you want like a pro. It's like dreaming of the perfect beach bod. Unless you're willing to go to the gym regularly to build it, that and modifying your diet, you're simply *in love* with the idea.

Having a desire without following it through with the action it takes to make it happen will get you nowehere. That's being in love with the idea of getting. It's not hard to see that wanting ain't enough, like I said eralier. If you just want without working for it, you'll remain where you are. Intent alone, is not enough. Be it asking for a deal, a break, a date or a multitude of other limitless life and business agreements and possibilities, what you tell yourself, and do as a result (the associated action), will either lead you to failure or to success. Only after negotiating positively with yourself can you move on to negotiating with others. The first person you must positively influence, is you. And guess what? You have the power of influence over yourself, so getting to a 'yes' with yourself is entirely up to you.

Choose your best state of mind first

Motivational speakers like Tony Robbins and many others, including myself, preach that once you change your state of mind, you change your outcome. Being in the right state of mind improves your life spirit, and, as a great bonus, your circumstances and outcomes. It also makes you feel in control, providing you with a powerful energy. How you choose to use that energy is limitless. It's really up to you.

Changing your state is easily accomplished by what you convince yourself of, through, for one, the practice of mantras. To get the best out of this, your whole physiology must be a play to generate the belief and results you're after for yourself. Express your mantras using your body *and* your tone of voice. Write them down and commit them to a journal[4] or a promise sheet. Once you do, dance in front of a mirror and shout them out! Who the heck cares?! Doing so will help you believe what you're telling yourself in your exercise to create that positive state of mind. The more you do it, the easier it becomes. Just like asking and negotiating. It's that easy.

When you reach positive agreements consistently within yourself first, you'll be in a much better state of mind to exude value to your negotiatee's, aligning you perfectly to help get you what you ask for – and at no loss of value to either of you. Remember that getting what you want in your ask or negotiation is an exchange, so they'll get something too. Once you master two-way negotiating, you'll naturally get more out of life - guaranteed.

---

[4] An excellent journal that encourages mantras, self-examination and a number of other life-changing positive habits is "The 'It's my life' journal" by J. Paul Nadeau

***

Dance and sing out your mantras and see
just how powerfully your state of mind
changes. Should anyone happen to see
you, invite them to join in.

***

All this means is that by having the right state of mind accompanied by the right techniques, others will *want* to listen to what you have to say, and they'll seriously consider granting what you ask for. Magic? No: Method.

That doesn't mean you'll always get you're after, but it sure does mean you'll get what you're after more often when you use the principles' you're about to discover in PIER™ Negotiating. We're all naturally and inherently programmed to be attracted to energetic and confident people – *charismatic,* dependable, trustworthy, action-based magnets, so to speak - especially when we know they aren't out to get us. Helping you discover how to develop these essential negotiating and asking skills is the intent of this book.

Make positive self-chatter your new habit

We all talk to ourselves, be it in thought or out loud; whether positively or negatively. Indeed, the most life-impactful and life-changing conversations we'll ever have are the ones we'll have, and do have, with **ourselves**. Those we have with others are secondary conversations. We must make each of our primary and secondary conversations matter however; the first ones will be the ones we have with ourselves while considering how to approach our negotiatee later. The latter ones will focus on our negotiatee first and foremost (at first[5]), especially if our intent is to positively influence a change in their behavior. I'll explain this in much greater detail as we go on.

Unstoppable self-chatter: yours and mine

Everybody you pass by in the street, sit across from on the subway, or watch in a café are all going through silent monologues in their heads, debating this and that, telling themselves good and bad things, or arguing an internal storm within. Some do so out loud. I know I do when I'm alone. But here's something you should know: those who get the most out of life are the ones who have discovered how to control that self-chatter: how to talk to themselves positively, each and every day, to boost themselves up and go for what they want, and they've made their positive self-talk a habit. They realize they are the directors of their own lives and choices, and they envision the very best outcomes for themselves, every time.

And because we are more similar than we are different, and we are the directors of *our* own lives, we can – and must - do the very same. No matter whether it's a thought or a storm, our self-talks are quite often the preludes to the secondary conversations we'll have with others that will follow and they'd better be damn good.

To get more out of life, our primary monologues must always be empowering, focused and self-constructive. Later, to influence behavior and collaboration with others, we'll focus on our negotiatees and their wants and needs at first, asking for what we want only once the time and conditions are right. Only by un-hostaging and building ourselves up can we reach our most

---

[5] I say at 'first' because the natural evolvement of doing so helps us get what we want

confident and powerful states, thereby providing us with what we need to forge ahead along the PIER™ and get more out life.

The power of an acronym

I'm a keynote speaker. I entered this profession after delivering a TEDx talk in 2015 on the topic of 'Finding Humanity Amid Terrorism and Global Unrest[6]'. As I began delivering keynote talks thereafter on the topic of negotiating for success in life and in business, it occurred to me that if I came up with a memorable acronym for the key points I was delivering, it would significantly help my audiences remember my negotiation principles more easily. PIER™® was born from that desire to provide my audiences with principles they could easily recall and immediately use through the acronym. PIER™ has been the bedrock on which I laid each negotiation principle out for my audiences, and it will be the bedrock I'll lay out for you here.

The **P** in **PIER™** stands for **Planning**. Planning is the winners' blueprint. Planning is an absolute must to help us solidify our every-day life and professional successes. Without planning, we sacrifice our outcomes to mere and unreliable chance. We are planners by nature. We plan what to wear, what to eat, how to get to work, school and countless other daily tasks. We plan big life events too – like weddings, job interviews and so much more. You have a much greater chance of getting the results you're after when you **plan first**. If you're to succeed more often in your life and business negotiations, then you must make planning one of your utmost priorities – along with every other principle in PIER™. Planning matters to success – without it, you leave the outcome to mere chance. That's why 'Planning' got first place in my acronym. I'll show you how to plan exceptionally well as we go along.

---

[6]YouTube – TEDx Toronto, Finding humanity amid terrorism and global unrest

The **I** in **PIER™** stands for **Intention**. Intention is a decision to act or behave in a specific way. Intention is not enough on its own – it must be demonstrated through action and behavior. The two work as a team. In all your negotiations, having the right intention (along with a demonstration of such) will provide you with more positive outcomes, more trust from your negotiatee's, stronger relationships, more successes and a more rewarding life. Never ignore the value of intention followed by the corresponding actions. A purely *self-focused* intention – which I recommend you never use, will be seen for what it is: purely *self*-focused. People will know when you make it "all about you."

By making it all about you, eventually, that approach will bring you nothing but loss and quite possibly, shattered and irreparable relationships, not to mention the possibility of severe reputation damage. It will certainly kill your professional negotiation deals, your relationships and much more, whereas having the right intention and corresponding action will reward you in kind. The right or wrong intention will come out in your body language, your tone of voice, your words, your behavior and the very attitude (the "vibrations") you convey. It *will* affect your outcome.

The **E** in **PIER™** stands for **Entrance** and **Engagement**. What do I mean by *entrance* and *engagement*? What I mean, for one, is that *first* impression you make when meeting someone for the first time. Your stage entrance, if you will: how you handle yourself in those first few important moments of that life or business negotiation. Those first milliseconds will have a tremendous impact on what comes next in PIER™.

People judge us in but a few milliseconds of meeting us, so we'd better plan to use those precious few milliseconds carefully to make the absolute best 'first' impression we possibly can. That's the '**entrance**'; next comes **engagement**: how you handle yourself throughout your encounter and how you engage with your negotiatee once you've made your very best first impression. Both will hugely influence what comes next: The **R** in **PIER™**...

The **R** in **PIER™** stands for **Relationship**. As a progression through the PIER™, having planned for your first meeting, having chosen the right intention, having made your best first impression and engaged meaningfully throughout, you are now on your way to building the relationship.

Now I know I talk about 'firsts,' but it need not be your first meeting with your negotiatee. You can use the PIER™ at any time – even to recover from failed firsts. It's never too late to stand by the PIER™. In fact, with failed firsts, you must.

If you *truly* want what you're after; if you *truly* want what you're entitled to and deserve, then you'd be wise to work on developing strong, positive, and lasting relationships. Create them. Getting what you want in life **and** in business depends on how well you build and treat your relationships. Relationships matter. When solid relationships are created, asking for commitments comes easy.

So, there you have it: a brief overview of **PIER™** negotiating. It won't be hard to master the PIER™ Principles or the guideposts associated with them - the rewards for doing so will be well worth the investment of your time.

PART 2

GIVE THEM REASONS TO SAY YES

Chapter Two

FOUNDATION BUILDING

S he's gone to be with the angels" are not the words a hostage negotiator wants to hear when he or she is negotiating with a suicidal man, who, just hours earlier, had broken into his estranged wife's home, violently removed her and barricaded himself inside with their two-year-old daughter. My heart pounded excruciatingly louder with each passing second as I tried to make sense of what I'd just heard. I turned off my microphone momentarily, took a deep breath, refocused on the task at hand and moved forward. On went the microphone again following that brief instant of fear and uncertainty; I knew I had to forge ahead, despite what I'd just been told. Did what he just say mean what I feared it meant? Was this innocent child…gone?

Let me back up a moment. I'd been handed the call two hours earlier. A distressed and suicidal man, separated from his wife for only a few weeks, had returned to the matrimonial home and abducted their child, holding her hostage inside as he contemplated his fate – and that of his daughters. He'd mentioned killing them all more than once and a police restraining order had been placed on him. I need not state the obvious: this is one of the many times a legal document serves little in assuring safety and peace.

From all accounts, he loved his daughter. This I knew from the ongoing intelligence I was receiving throughout the negotiation. I knew he'd been a good father to his little girl, and that was one of the golden hooks I chose to use throughout my negotiation with him. "What will Camille think if you take your life, Jacques?" "*Are* you considering killing yourself?"

As a negotiator, there can be no room for vague, unspecific language. In no negotiation, for that matter. We must use direct, and often ugly language, even when it feels uncomfortable to do so, so there can be absolutely no room for misunderstanding. Asking a suicidal person that direct question serves one of two purposes: the first is to shock them. It's one thing to think about killing yourself (and/or another) and a totally different thing to voice it out when someone calls you on it, in this case, a hostage negotiator. The second is for the benefit of all team members assigned to the negotiation; from Incident Commander to Secondary Negotiators, to the Tactical Unit and everyone else in between. We need to know what we're up against at all times. Only then can we know in which direction to proceed. This applies as much to you as it does to any hostage negotiator.

Getting back to Jacques, who spoke English with a thick Québécois accent: he'd lost his job, turned to booze and became increasingly aggressive toward his wife. His violent and unpredictable behavior had led her to do what begged and needed to be done: have him removed from the home for her safety and that of their child's, and to involve the police.

I initiated the negotiation in text-book fashion and maintained a flow of professionalism throughout. He was pouring his heart out to me, listening and eventually agreeing with me, through what seemed like genuine, heart-felt tears. I saw his point of view first, earned the right to express mine and we connected. We had agreed on an exit strategy. He no longer wanted to kill himself or Camille. He was ready to come out peaceably. "Ok Jacques, the tactical officers are just outside the front door. We've gone through this. Don't be alarmed. They won't hurt you. Make your way outside now and just follow their instructions." "Just one minute, Paul. I want to check on Camille before I go out," was his reply. "Jacques, no. Listen to me. She's fine. Camille is fine. Come out now. We'll check on her the moment you leave the house. I promise. It's going to be OK."

He dropped the phone suddenly and I struggled for what seemed like minutes at a decision I had to make within just a few seconds: whether to call an assault on the house and use whatever force necessary to stop Jacques from taking a step further toward his daughter, or to wait. I knew that even if I called it, the tactical officers would not likely reach her bedroom in time. No one had a clear shot, I'd been told. His sudden departure from our agreement was unexpected and left me wondering what had gone wrong. 'He assured me he wouldn't harm his daughter or himself' is what swirled through my head as I repeatedly called his name over the phone in hopes he had not moved far from the line and could still hear my voice. Moments later, he returned to the phone. "She's gone to be with the angels, Paul. It's over." He abruptly hung up the phone. I shouted out, "We need an immediate dynamic entry!" The tach officers immediately burst in. I then bowed my head as tears started to swell up in my eyes. I'd lost this precious child. I should have called it earlier.

What had gone wrong? I'd followed the negotiators text-book to the letter and had built a solid foundation with Jacques. He'd come to know me, like me and trust me. I was beyond myself. I was in shock. My evaluator put his hand on my shoulder and dropped his other hand, holding his clipboard and evaluation sheet to his side. "I didn't see that coming either, Paul," is all he said, in a reassuring voice. Yes, my evaluator.

This was NOT an actual hostage negotiation, but an exercise on which I was being graded for my final test at the Canadian Police College in order to receive my qualification as a certified hostage and crisis negotiator. The Canadian Police College use experienced improvisational actors to play the roles of hostage takers and to make the negotiation unfold as real as possible. These improv actors are not told how the exercise ends, just that they react according to how the negotiator is handling his or her negotiation. By what had just happened, it appeared I'd failed. Big time. And it wasn't over just yet. Much to my chagrin, I now had to face Jacques - with the thick French accent - for a debriefing and to find out where I'd gone so horribly wrong.

Although this was simply an exercise in role-play, every second of it felt as real as it gets, for both Jacques and me. To immerse yourself fully into role-play such as this is an all-important key in the preparation phase of any negotiation. It prepares you for just about anything that may come along. *Just about everything*. Role-play or not, I had a strong urge to pummel the shit out of Jacques the moment I met him. It felt that real to me.

As I walked down the hall accompanied by my evaluator, I saw him walking toward me. A man in his mid to late 20's, he looked like 'Weird Al Yankovic,' the singer-songwriter satirist: long wavy black hair, goofy glasses, thin build and sporting a smile from ear to ear. 'A smile from ear to ear?!' is all I could think of when I first saw him. How dare he smile. I was fuming.

Jacques reached me, pointed at me, shook his head from left to right and said, "Paul, Paul!" I didn't say a word. I just stood there, fuming, still in shock, I imagine. "You got me! You talked me out!"

he said. I still said nothing. "She's *not* gone to be with the angels. I couldn't do it. I was going to come out, but then thought, damn, *no one's* ever talked me out!" He looked at my evaluator, and it was clear to me that the two men knew each other well. This was not Jacques' first rodeo. He'd been doing this for two years. Addressing my evaluator, he continued, "PIER™, I was just messing with him. *He* did it. He talked me out and Camille is safe. That's a first, and I've got to admit, it feels good." Now I just wanted to smack him about the head and body in three ways: fast, hard and continuously, but an overwhelming sense of relief came over me suddenly and I figured beating the shit out of him would score me no good points in my evaluation.

Interestingly, the relief that came over me was not due to his disclosure or that it meant I would pass my practical exercise; it came over me because Camille was alive, and he'd been talked out, safely. Weird, isn't it? I finally shook Jacques hand. Well, that was my first graded practical exercise and I had passed it. Now let me fill you in on how I got to that stage and beyond.

My journey to negotiating

For me, negotiating started early in life in my fledgling attempts to negotiate with my grade school teachers in *not* giving me the strap for my unruly behavior in class and with my father in not giving me a beating. I suspect the reason I was so unruly in grade school was my reaction and defense to the abuse I experienced at home.

When I was twelve years old, my father sent me out to find a part-time job so I could pay for my keep – room and board, as he saw it. Despite being as young and inexperienced as I was, I found myself negotiating with grown-ups to get a job in order to meet his demands. My paper route had not been enough. I observed, learned and practiced the asking and negotiation skills I needed to get what

I was after. I taught myself how to negotiate, and trial, error, and practice amounted to more than one success for me over time. Eventually, I nailed negotiating and asking. Knowing how to do so professionally became invaluable to me. Enjoying the process made it that much easier and rewarding.

After joining the police at the age of twenty-one, I successfully negotiated for more exciting jobs. Once I'd been promoted to the rank of detective, I used my finely developed skills to negotiate confessions from criminals. Yes, I use the word 'negotiate' because many of the principles used in negotiation are also used in interrogation, and in almost every other human interaction you'll ever have.

My journey began by negotiating to satisfy my fathers' demands – negotiating for survival. Next, I negotiated for jobs and outcomes; for better opportunities (profit) and finally to help others. It's been an exciting journey with a myriad of rewards.

We got our asses kicked at first

Before I delve more thoroughly into the principles of PIER™ Negotiating, it might help if I share with you *how* the right negotiating principles were reached, because the wrong way of doing things just couldn't go on. By shedding some light on that, you'll see why the approach I offer in the pages of this book will also work for you. You may relate to how it 'used' to be done and immediately see the benefits of how it's 'now' done.

The hostage and crisis negotiating techniques in use today were developed over years of tried and true practice by the very negotiators assigned to do the job. These techniques are products of experimental learning and discovery and have been modified and improved with the input of learned psychiatrists and an array of specialists who have studied human behavior and discovered why people behave the way they do. These much-needed modifications and improvements to the approach of how hostage negotiations were being conducted were reached through copious amounts of discussion, observation, dissection and tried experience; by picking apart what went well and what did not. The 'way it used to be done' kicked our asses more than once and forced positive change to take place. Sometimes all you need to do is examine what's not going right and modify it until you get it right.

We went from screwing things up to getting it right

Hostage negotiations have been around since the beginning of recorded time. Historical fiction is regaled with accounts of pirates engaging in the not-so-subtle 'negotiations' for 'booty' in exchange for 'life.' From seas to the jungles, capturing hostages for ransom has sadly become a profitable business, one which regrettably still lives on to this day.

I have no intention to turning this into a history lesson, but the following will help you understand how we got to where we are now.

Following the brutal taking and handling of several hostages over a number of days in a bank in Stockholm, Sweden, in 1973, police and psychologists observed the psychological effect some hostages suffered under extreme pressure, now referred to as the Stockholm syndrome: a phenomenon in which a hostage demonstrably develops identification with, and empathy for, their hostage-taker. That discovery, among a host of other tangential discoveries, was instrumental in comprehending the social aberration tersely known as 'Waco,' which ultimately resulted in the deaths of numerous hostages (who did *not* realize or consider themselves hostages) – including their leader, David Koresh[7].

Indeed, the Waco anomaly was one of many instances that reaffirmed the use of an approach in negotiations that takes into serious consideration emotion 'client-based' techniques. This aforementioned snippet on the Stockholm syndrome is an important piece because many of us succumb to this mentality ourselves by choice when we hostage ourselves to unhealthy pasts, thoughts, limitations or relationships.

As a matter of record, the primary negotiator in the Waco fiasco was an FBI Negotiator by the name of Gary Noesner, who is now an acquaintance of mine. Agent Noesner handled himself and the negotiation professionally throughout his involvement. It was no easy task, as all who are familiar with the Waco disaster know far too well. His techniques were directly in line with PIER™ Negotiating.

Regrettably, the impatience of his commanding tactical officers and the political idiots calling the shots throughout that disaster resulted in his removal from the negotiation far too prematurely and at a severe cost. They wanted 'quicker' results, which does not often happen in complicated negotiations. The results of rushing the *negotiation*, in this case, were catastrophic. That's why I'll be preaching a take-your-time whenever you can approach. We learned from the Waco disaster and many other failed negotiations, and you will too.

---

[7] David Koresh was the American leader of the Branch Davidians religious sect, believing himself to be its final prophet. https://en.wikipedia.org/wiki/David_Koresh

***

Life and experience have been some of the
hostage negotiators greatest teachers. By
examining what went wrong, we adjusted
our approach until we got things right. We
went from screwing things up to getting
things right.

***

Taking your time, sticking by the principles of PIER™ Negotiating you're about to discover and never rushing the negotiation will reap far greater rewards for you than trying to shortcut the process. Imagine Waco in your next complicated negotiation.

We've discovered a lot over the years. Along with the increasing need to develop and adopt more emotion-based techniques, there also evolved the realization and need to address the release of hostages without the use of force, coercion or loss of life. Patterning tools and techniques which emanate from the emotional content of danger-fraught situations which necessitate extremely diplomatic negotiation replaced the stiff, business-first *"You listen to me and do what I tell you to..."* approach, which hostage negotiators had previously been using so ineffectively. A welcomed and much-needed improvement for sure. Why didn't we figure this shit out earlier? Ego and power? Stuff like that will blow your success, and not in a good way.

The approach of patience, listening first and earning the right to present your point of view once you've understood theirs, works. This is the approach I implore you to adopt. To become a badass negotiator, you must first seek to understand, and then to be understood. You must consider the needs, wants and expectations of your negotiatee(s) first and foremost while never abandoning yours, naturally. To put your needs and wants first, you set yourself up to crash and burn.

One need only look at the current situation involving our on-going fight against terrorism, for example, to see that telling someone how to live their lives (or run their business), force values or expectations or our solutions on them can and likely will lead to severe consequences. I'm pleased to say that the approach we now use is largely a reversal to that stiff, outdated and ineffective, idiotic approach. Rather, we might now say something like: "Let me listen to *you* first," "What is it *you're* after?" or "How can we work this out, *together*?" - any of which works far more effectively than simply, crudely, commanding someone to do our will or see things our way.

Think of these discoveries as you read on and imagine how they might apply to your everyday life and business negotiations: to *your* world. The PIER™ approach to negotiating and asking embraces the theory of reciprocation and working on solutions *together*. That's what works, plain and simple.

Successful negotiations occur when the needs, expectations, fears, and concerns of the 'negotiatee' are considered and addressed first and foremost, and not just when the negotiator focuses on imposing his or her will above that of their negotiatee. This applies to any negotiation – yours included, be it with a vendor, a spouse, a child, parent or whomever. Everyone needs to feel heard, appreciated, understood and validated.

The similarities between "life" and hostage negotiations

By now you may be wondering what hostage negotiations and your life negotiations have in common. You may be considering your own negotiations and imagining how to apply the benefits of what you've read so far and what you're about to read to your circumstances. So, what *do* they have in common?

For years hostage negotiators approached negotiations in the same way many businesses and life negotiators still regularly approach their negotiations today – all business (or in the case of an intimate relationship, the use of power and control and/or the lack of personal connection), and omitting 'positive' bridge building relationship musts. That "You listen to me" approach was much the former way of doing things in hostage negotiations. It was the way my troubled father approached all of us – his family. That approach builds walls and fear – not bridges, respect, love and cooperation.

And as for the hostage negotiators of yesteryear? There was little planning involved or consideration for the emotional being they were negotiating with, and the negotiators wanted their voices to be heard, and demands to be met above all else, first and foremost. Consequently, in hostage situations, many lives were lost by the application of this tough, one-sided, unilateral approach.

Through a stream of public indictments and conduct reviews, it became apparent that we had to change our approach drastically if we were to help save lives. If you have a "listen to me first" approach to your important life and business negotiations, or if your approach is cold and impersonal, you may not be risking a life, but you'll certainly be jeopardizing opportunities to enrich your life and that of your negotiatee's and you'll be kissing your chances of sealing whatever deal you're after 'goodbye.'

By forcing your ideas and/or solutions on another or dismissing those of the one you should be considering in the negotiation, you'll lose their respect and quite possibly the relationship, not to mention the deal. There are consequences to the use of force and intimidation.

There are more similarities than differences in all negotiations

Now I'll admit that life, business and hostage negotiations are different negotiations; but they are negotiations, nevertheless; they involve communication and agreement seeking, and there are principles and techniques hostage negotiators use today that can and will help you succeed in all your life and business interactions. There are more similarities in effective negotiating than there are differences.

Thankfully, the way it used to be is gradually and slowly changing because we're now getting more twenty to thirty-year- old business owners and entrepreneurs who are adapting to the new way of getting what they want as they soak in the many incredibly informative articles on relationship building. LinkedIn is filled with 'how to succeed in business' tips and articles and most of those articles focus on building relationships. They take the relationship building aspect of business and negotiations seriously. It's the way to go. To ignore the primary importance of establishing the relationship is tantamount to achieving a less than optimal outcome in any/all negotiations, whatever type they may be. I'll be discussing much more on relationships later. It is, after all, the "R" in PIER™.

***
Successful negotiations occur when the
needs, expectations, fears, and concerns of
the 'negotiatee' are considered and
addressed first and foremost, and not just
when the negotiator focuses on imposing
his or her will above that of their
negotiatee.
***

Business bulletin # 1: It's in the details – or is it? Examining Differences *and* Similarities in business and hostage negotiations

For the business professional who has embarked on this journey at my earlier invitation, let's look at some of the main differences between business and hostage negotiations. The purpose of this exploration is to quite simply point out that in almost every negotiation, there are more similarities than there are differences. This is why our 'hostage and crisis' negotiation methods, and more specifically, the PIER™ principles you're being introduced to apply so well to *your world* as well as they do to all others. Once we've examined the main differences, we can then explore similarities throughout this book.

Hey, even if you don't consider yourself a *business* negotiator, I urge you to follow along. You'll see how this vital information applies to your world of life negotiations just as much.

A hostage negotiation *is* a crisis negotiation

Alright, let me begin by admitting the obvious: a hostage negotiation *is* a crisis negotiation. Admittedly, it is distinct in content from the business negotiation, most day-to-day life negotiations, an entertainment contract negotiation - or any other negotiation for that matter. But each negotiation, regardless of what kind, share a multitude of similarities, and the principles outlined in this book that work exceptionally well in hostage and crisis negotiations *will* work in all your life and business negotiations just as effectively.

Obviously, adjustments must be considered and made depending on who you're negotiating with, what state they're in and what's at stake. But make no mistake - hostage negotiation principles work in *all* negotiations. They take into consideration that the negotiatee is an emotional being. This must be considered in each of your negotiations as well, whether you're negotiating with the neighborhood shopkeeper or a CEO of a large corporation.

One of the main differences between a hostage negotiation and a business negotiation is that the hostage negotiator can't walk away from their negotiation; whereas *you* can. Hostage negotiators can't settle for "most" of what we came to get; for example, for freeing two out of four hostages. We can't go in with the mindset that if we get two out of four hostages, it's been a good day. No. It must be four out of four. Can you imagine if a hostage negotiator would say, "Well Bill, I see we can't agree on shit. Okay, you keep the hostages. Sorry we couldn't reach an agreement." No, that just can't happen. You cannot leave a crisis or negotiation of any kind before you've exhausted all possibilities of an agreeable outcome.

Additionally, in a crisis or hostage negotiation, there's 'no time to plan,' whereas you can. It's not as though the hostage-takers called well in advance to tell us of their plans. In business negotiations, you *can* walk away and sometimes, you MUST. In some life negotiations, not so easily (if you want the outcome to work in both your favor badly enough that is, especially in intimate relationships).

In your case, granted, I understand that you're not negotiating to save a life, but you are negotiating a deal or intent of some sort that is significantly important to you. Hostage negotiators must *care* about the outcome; whereas in business negotiations, for example, you really don't.

Hostage negotiators don't, however, focus on the *outcome* immediately. We focus on the process first, and we don't walk away until it has been exhaustively completed (a similarity). That could take hours or days, but hostage negotiators cannot - and will not walk away before completion, whereas, you can.

What you came for or what you entered the negotiation to reach is extremely important, of course; but you *can* walk away from it at any time if it isn't working out for you. And sometimes you absolutely must. You don't have to "care" about the *outcome* as much as a hostage negotiator does. And you must care enough about yourself to know if you're getting a good deal or if you're about to lose too much. Same applies to life. Care about them, care about you. Know when to walk away.

***

Focusing on your end goal is not the way to go. Focus, rather, on the process of getting you there. Doing so allows you to be present in each moment and encourages you to work at understanding your negotiatees wants and needs. It also opens the door for you to make your proposal with more chances of getting a 'yes' when the time is right.

***

Don't care about the outcome of your negotiation — for real

Here's a twist you might have just clued into that I'm going to ask you to consider: I'm asking you to consider taking an *"I don't care about the **outcome**"* approach in your business negotiations. Let me make this clear. I'm referring to business negotiations and not your intimate relationships, obviously. Not that you *won't* care about the outcome or do your very best to get the best outcome for yourself - of course not. It's simply that I ask that your approach shift from being focused on arriving at where you want to be to being focused on the journey of getting to where you want to be. Imagine the image of a PIER™ in your mind. One that looks over a vast, beautiful sea. Don't focus on where you want to end up going, focus on the unlimited possibilities and wonders of getting there. The journey is often much more exciting than arriving to your destination.

Consider, if you will, a Captain of a ship or a jet plane. They know where they want to go but they must first focus on arriving there safely and deal with weather, winds, unexpected bumps or whatever they encounter along the way. They work in 'the now,' not in 'the results.' Much as you must in your negotiation. There's seldom a straight line to your outcome or destination.

By not *dwelling* on the outcome, you remain more focused on the process and your negotiatee's needs first. The rest will unfold naturally. Take your eyes off the prize, at first. Never feel pressured to settle at your expense. Care about the person and the process of getting to what you want, but don't be so invested in the outcome that you say 'Yes' when you ought to be saying "No." "No" is, after all, something you have the right to say as much as your negotiatee has. "Yes" is even better. But "No" is where each negotiation begins.

***
Remain alert and never feel pressured into
accepting anything that doesn't work for
you. Remember that you can always walk
away from any negotiation if you need to.
***

From contrast to similarity

Many business negotiations focus on intellectual power, rational
notions of value in what is fair and what is not, following scripts,
presenting offers and counter-offers and blah-de-dah, all the while
often neglecting the importance of the relationship. They're often
absent of understanding and actively listening to the person being
negotiating with. Do that and you'll miss out on making so much
happen for yourself. Just because that may have been the way to do
it in the past doesn't mean it should be done today.

Successful negotiations, on the other hand, are about connecting
with the person across from you, listening, being open to their needs
and ideas, establishing trust and rapport, and expressing solutions
once you completely understand your negotiatee's needs, concerns,
and desires. Only then can you present your best solutions
confidently, and work with your negotiatee to reach an agreement
that works for both of you. Effective negotiation is about making an
impression that leaves the other feeling, "I know him/her, I like
him/her, and I trust him/her, and this *is* the person I want to say yes
to."

Everybody wants to feel acknowledged, heard and understood. Just
check Facebook and Instagram for proof of that. Listening is one of
the most effective means of establishing connection. This works as
effectively in your life negotiations as it does in business. Adopt the

20/80% rule: do 20% of the talking and 80% of the listening. Many negotiators don't spend the time needed to truly 'listen' and understand their negotiatees' needs.

Many people trying to connect in life make the same mistake. They talk too much in the beginning, making it about what *they want* or about themselves first. Or that first little while is spent talking about how great they *think* they are. How would that go on a first date? Can you relate to a date or meeting in which that very thing happened? How long were you 'impressed'?

The reason for this misguided approach is that the inexperienced negotiator is either not motivated or trained enough to listen *with the soul* first, and that's a critical shortcoming. I'll explain what I mean by 'listen with the soul' as you read on. For now, understand that success is reached by making a connection, and you accomplish that more effectively by expressing genuine interest in the other person instead of trying to impress them with your vision of how great you are.

Don't get me wrong: you may very well be great – and what you have to offer may be exactly what they need (remember, you may be their answer), but let them discover this on their own, slowly, as trust and interest are

Everybody wants to be acknowledged, heard and understood. Listening is one of the most effective means of establishing that connection.

developed. You'll know when and how much to talk about yourself and what you have to offer up as time goes on. As rapport is built, they'll feel comfortable asking you questions and the 'exchange' begins.

New and improved negotiations: the right approach to successful influence

Another difference between most life, business and hostage negotiations is approach and the anticipation of human nature. A hostage negotiator anticipates how people will behave, keeping human needs and desires in mind given whatever circumstance we encounter. We understand that in order to succeed, we must always treat our negotiatee with dignity and respect, considering their feelings and interests. Only then will they be willing to reciprocate.

"Hostage negotiators understand the importance of developing strong interpersonal relationships. The psychology considers emotions, emotional intelligence and understanding, then deploys tactics to calm individuals in states of crisis, establish rapport, gain trust, get them talking and verbalizing their needs and move them to a place where they feel you're really listening *and* empathizing with them, working toward solutions and outcomes together[8]".

We move the hostage-taker to a point where he/she believes that he/she is the one who came up with the best solution for himself/herself (with a bit of direction from us, of course). They feel they were a big part of arriving at an amicable solution and thereby are happy to take ownership of it.

People feel much better when they feel that they've come up with the best solution on their own, even though you've been extremely instrumental through exploratory discovery and dialogue in helping them reach it. Telling someone how to feel or giving them your solution first without listening to them is not the correct approach. In fact, it will likely piss them off and they'll be through listening to you.

---

[8] Chris Voss – Never split the difference ©2016 HarperCollins Publishers

Most people often know the answer to their distress or what's bothering them and simply need to be heard as they express their feelings or figure it out on their own as they verbalize what's bothering them.

But far too often, some of us give our 'advice,' solutions or opinions when the best thing we could ever do is shut the hell up, to listen solefully and empathize first. The recipe for listening and empathizing works in hostage negotiating - and works effectively at getting the hostage taker to give up without harming their hostages. This recipe will also work in your world, no matter what kind of negotiation you find yourself in.

Empathy is understanding the feelings and mindset of the other person in the moment and also hearing what is behind those emotions so that you can increase your influence in all those moments and the moments that follow. It's bringing your attention to both the emotional obstacles and the potential pathways to getting an agreement done.

Empathy is a classic, soft communication skill. When we closely observe a person's face, gestures and tone of voice our brain begins to align with theirs. This allows us to understand more of what they're thinking and feeling. It's observing body language and reading body language to your advantage. Empathy helps us learn the position of the person sitting across from us - what may be bothering them, what position they're in, and what might move them forward. As negotiators we use empathy because it works.

"Hostage negotiators understand the importance of developing strong interpersonal relationships. The psychology considers emotions, emotional intelligence and understanding, then deploys tactics to calm individuals in states of crisis, establish rapport, gain trust, get them talking and verbalizing their needs and move them to a place where they feel you're really listening and empathizing with them, working toward solutions and outcomes 'together.'
Chris Voss – "Never split the difference"

We solidify the feeling of empathy by asking questions; by showing genuine interest in the other person and by listening with our souls. It's only when these steps are taken that the *best* deal, understanding and agreements can be reached. We don't tell them what to do; we listen and get them talking. It's an evolving process that may take time, but neglecting any step of the negotiation process as outlined here in this book jeopardizes your chances of success and those "Ah ha! Yes, that's it, that's the solution for me!" moments, no matter who you're negotiating with.

Now doesn't that make sense for your life and business negotiations as well? Considering emotions, emotional intelligence, and understanding? Involving the other individual and listening to them first? Making the other individual feel heard and understood? I, for one, know it does because I've witnessed first-hand how effectively doing so works. It's in large part what has granted me so many successes. This approach is what gets you the best results. Remember that everybody has an innate desire to be heard and understood – people don't like to be told what to do or how to think, but we can gently guide and influence them into seeing a much better picture, if only we listen with the intent to understand first.

***
People will shut you down in a New York
minute if they don't feel you care enough to
listen.
***

The importance of involving your negotiatee in reaching solutions: without them, there is no negotiation

Business Bulletin # 2: Returning briefly to the business negotiation, sometimes it will become necessary to rescue your negotiatees from themselves, and you'll be surprised at how often they don't quite know what the right solution is, but may *think* they do.

Clarify what they hope to solve by asking *exploratory* questions/dialogue. Exploratory questions are exactly that: questions and dialogue that explores the needs and wants of the negotiatee, and more. It is vitally important to first explore what problems they're hoping to solve with your product or service and what results they're expecting to find. "What is it you hope to accomplish with this?" is a great start. Solutions must solve something; and your job will be to find the right solution for that desired result by using exploratory dialogue – by asking the *right* questions.

There will be times your negotiatees won't know what's best for them. If they can get you talking about your solution immediately, they're really taking the monkey off their backs and putting it smack dab on yours. But that monkey ain't tame yet. By doing that, they can sit back and just listen to you trying to solve their needs without, at times, really understanding what they are. It can easily become a one-person circus then, with you as the main entertainment. And that doesn't make much sense now, does it? You're at a complete disadvantage without having all the facts. And where do you get the facts? From them.

It's the very same in life. The idea is to involve your negotiatee in the process of reaching the best solution through exploratory dialogue. Find out exactly what it is that they're looking to solve and what results they're looking to find, and how you might help provide the best solution. Involving them in the process makes the process that much more meaningful. They become invested and engaged. Besides, it sends a message to them that you're genuinely interested in helping find a solution that's best for them and that you're listening. Move off the solution at first and ask exploratory questions. This is how you gather the facts that will help you in pitching your solution when the time is right. You'll see how this all works out in an upcoming story I'll be telling you.

For now, imagine this with your loved ones. How well would any significant interaction go if you didn't listen to them first, but simply provided your solution right off the bat, as *you* saw it? Most of us don't listen first – or listen well. Everybody has an inherent need to be heard and understood first. It's who we are.

By involving your negotiatee in the process, you are not babbling to deaf ears

Drawing upon my own experiences as a hostage negotiator and professional criminal interrogator, I discovered that, to be successful, I had to negotiate and interrogate in my negotiatees' world - and that meant involving them in the process. I discovered that it wasn't all about me and what I wanted. I needed to listen and understand my negotiatees' point of view first. I needed to see through their eyes to understand their perspectives and fears first if I was ever to succeed in getting what I was after. I couldn't simply guess what they were. I had to ask what they were. Without that, I couldn't possibly expect to know what words to use that would motivate or influence my negotiatee enough to trust me and allow me the right to propose the best solution for them – and for *us*.

Imagine this if you will: what I had to offer them they wanted no part of at first. What criminal under investigation for a serious crime, in his or her right mind, would be anxious to confess and say 'Yes' to a police detective, knowing full well that a confession meant they were going to jail? Or a hostage-taker whose day went from bad to worse after an uninvited negotiator showed up to the disaster fiasco and added even more stress to their already stress-filled nightmare?

For me, success came after I set aside my personal objectives. It came when we each understood what the real issues were and how we could work *together* in finding the best solution. I *chose* not to approach any situation with a predetermined judgment of the other person or his/her needs, or with the intent of *telling* them what they needed to do or suggest that I magically had the solution. How could I know what the best or right solution was without hearing from them first? That makes absolutely no sense.

Let's now examine the approach. I begin with a story I just told you I'd tell of a client who was offered a better solution than the one he'd originally considered.

Saying no to a Prince

It's quite alright to suggest something your negotiatee may not have considered. In fact, it makes perfect business and life sense, especially if it's the best solution.

An acquaintance of mine once told me a story involving the now sadly departed music legend, 'Prince.' Prince, who had a home in Toronto, Canada, called a popular music store my acquaintance was managing in Toronto to buy some musical instrument attachment. The manager (my acquaintance) was informed what Prince wanted to buy and he instructed the salesperson who answered Prince's call to tell Prince that they weren't going to sell it to him. As you can well imagine, Prince wasn't too pleased with that original 'No' and asked to speak to the man who was refusing to sell it to him.

Following a very brief telephone conversation with the manager, Prince was provided solid reasons why it wasn't the best fit for him, and he was offered another instrument that would best suit his needs. Most importantly, he involved Prince in the process. Once they explored the reasons that it was a better fit for him, Prince happily bought the suggested instrument attachment instead.

The story doesn't end there. Prince was so impressed that he invited the manager to his home for a social visit; and from that point on, the two developed a very profitable business relationship. The store manager was invited more than once to Prince's home for social events, and that led to more sales for that music store as well as a solid business relationship with a super-star.

What lessons can you draw from this simple story?
- For one, understand that the ability to *connect* with your negotiatee is the first step in forming a relationship which, in turn, is an important step in the process of successful negotiation. Consider your negotiatee and what's best for them first.

- Involve your negotiatee in the process. Not involving them is detrimental to positive outcomes.

- In some instances, your negotiatee may not know what solution is best for them – or they think they do. If you can provide a better solution, don't be afraid to suggest it. Involve them in the process.

In every successful negotiation, your task will be to ask exploratory questions to establish clarity and certainty. In business, for example, you'll want to ascertain that what your clients or prospective clients are asking for is going to provide them with the precise solution they're looking for. In life negotiations, you'll want to use the same approach.

As such, consider questions such as:

- What are you looking for in your ideal XYZ?

- What do you see as your ideal outcome in this negotiation/interaction?

- How can I help you reach the objectives you're after?

Only through exploration will you be able to determine if what you have to offer is what they need.

Guidepost number two: Dammit, Just ASK already!

"Dammit, Just Ask already!" is not only the title of this book, it's a central theme in the PIER™ approach to negotiating and asking, and it must become a freakin' habit. Getting what you want in life really is, *almost*, as simple as 'just asking' for it. I told you there was more to it

"You miss 100% of the shots you don't take."
~ Wayne Gretzky, Canadian hockey legend.

as you're discovering, otherwise why read this book, but you get the idea.

To be successful in asking, we must understand the *how, why* and *when* to ask. The three must be carefully considered. Negotiation success – as well as 'asking' success - evolves through effective communication, emotion, and relationship building. Neglecting any of these stages will jeopardize your right to ask successfully for what you want when it comes to the important stuff – the job, the date, the proposal or, in business, the deal, the extras.

What 'extras' do we ask for in a negotiation? For some of us, we begin by asking for the opportunity to meet. We ask for the other person's valuable time. We ask them to trust us enough to meet with us and hear us out; we even ask for them to share their fears and concerns to us; we later ask them to consider our solutions and proposals, and eventually, we ask for the agreement/commitment, whatever that is for us. Whew, that's a hell of a lot and if you mess up at any stage, you're out.

We must ask to get - not only for what we want but for the information and facts we need to help us understand and get there. Dammit, if you don't ask, you don't get. You miss 100% of the shots you don't take, after all.

I'll now provide you with a couple of personal examples on how "just asking" (using the PIER™ approach) worked exceptionally well for me.

After writing my first book, I looked for influential people to help me endorse it. I believe in the message of my book and I wanted to reach as many readers as possible. The importance of excellent endorsements in any undertaking is crucial, regardless of the business. Who to ask, I queried?

At the time, I'd been following Yannick Bisson[9] on Instagram and Twitter. Yannick is a very accomplished and popular Canadian film and television actor, known primarily for his role as 'Murdoch' on the 'Murdoch Mysteries'[10]. I like that show, and I admire Yannick's acting as well as the man himself, as do many others across the globe.

The rewards for asking are worth the asking. The rest is up to you to take it further, but the message here is simple: If you don't ask (correctly), you don't get.

I'd met Yannick very briefly once at a breakfast for ACTRA[11] actors in Toronto, Canada. I managed to introduce myself to him for a very brief moment in the foray of other ambitious actors, but that was the extent of my initial engagement with him. I later played a small role on one of the Murdoch Mysteries episodes in season eight of the show, but regrettably, I didn't get to work with him directly.

Now, a few years later, while pondering who to ask for endorsements, I tried reaching Yannick, twice. As luck would have it, I managed to connect with him the second time around, and after a brief re-introduction and setting out the purpose for my request, I 'just asked' if he would be interested in endorsing my book.

Now you may be asking, "But Paul, doesn't this contradict what you've told us about laying a foundation first, *before* asking?" Let me emphasize that when laying any foundation, it need not be a long, drawn-out process. In this case, through our correspondence, I was able to provide enough information to build that foundation – and value, as I saw it (and he as well, as it turned out). The

[9] Yannick Bisson
[10] The Murdoch Mysteries
[11] The Alliance of Canadian Cinema, Television and Radio Artists

foundation had been laid. We had once met, we were both actors, and the request was an honorable one. Yannick graciously accepted – it wasn't a 'jack-in-the-box' request.

If you ask without first providing sound reasons for a 'yes' to be granted, you'll rarely get what you're after. The rewards for asking are worth the asking. The rest is up to you to take it further, but the message here is simple: If you don't ask (correctly), you don't get.

My second example occurred in April 2012, when the world-famous Oprah Winfrey came to Toronto, Ontario on her "Life Class Tour." A dear friend of mine, Farah Bhanji, asked if I would volunteer with her at the event. We were both hoping to score sweet spots by the stage to catch the amazing speakers of the day, including Oprah herself and Tony Robbins. When the organizers handed out our assignments, poor Farah was going to be stationed two floors above the event guiding the attendees to the auditorium below, while I was given a spot *outside* the main auditorium, ticket collecting. Neither one of us were going to get to see any of the speakers that day.

About an hour before the attendees were permitted into the auditorium on the day of the event, I stepped into the auditorium to have a quick look around. I wanted to check it out, and I also had a plan (I'm a negotiator, after all – always thinking of how, by 'asking' correctly, my circumstances might improve).

I spotted the supervisor in charge of the main auditorium and she appeared understandably overwhelmed as she ruffled through her papers. So many seats and so few volunteers on the inside to help the crowds find their seats, I imagined. At least I hoped it was so.

Recognizing an opportunity before me, I approached her and identified the emotion I felt she was experiencing: "You look overwhelmed," I said. She nodded and answered, "Yes, I am. I have no idea how this is all going to work out." I followed with, "Do you have enough people to help you?" She answered, "No, I don't think so. I thought I did." Bingo! There was an opportunity unfolding before me to move to the next stage. One I had hoped for and needed to act upon immediately.

Having identified the need she had - I knew I had a solution for her. I had something of value to offer. As a retired policeman with over 31 years of experience on the job, I felt I would be a valuable asset to her and I told her about my credentials. "I think I can help you..." I opened with. I introduced myself by first name, shook her hand and told her a bit about myself.

After hearing my qualifications and how I believed I could help, she was more than delighted to have me join her team – in the auditorium, by the front stage! She said she would clear it with my supervisor. But I didn't stop there. My friend Farah was still two floors above us and I wanted her there too. I asked if Farah could join us and told my new supervisor why I felt Farah would be an additional asset. The deal was struck. Both Farah and I ended up working right by the stage and we got to hear all the wonderful speakers... and I even got to work directly with Oprah for 40 minutes as her personal bodyguard. We held hands at one point – but that's another story. Yeah, here it comes: If you don't ask, you don't get – you miss 100% of the shots you don't take.

When you recognize an opportunity, seize it. If you don't see one, create one. The worst anyone can say is 'No,' but as you see from this story, not only did I escape ticket collecting 'outside' of the main auditorium, I was stationed right by the main stage, and I later got to work directly with Oprah.

Now you may be thinking, "Yeah, but Paul... you had 31 years' experience as a cop. That's why she said yes to you." I can't disagree with that. You may be right. But even if I had not had 31 years' experience as a cop, I still would have asked and found something else of value to offer her. Think about what *you* have to offer your negotiatee – even if it's only a passionate willingness to help. Think deep: Using this example, for instance, maybe you once worked at a large event, a school event, or something else that might be a fit in the situation you find yourself in. And if not, again, what's the harm in asking? THERE IS NONE.

Exude passionately a confidence that you can help, no matter what you may or may not be bringing to the table. Remember, when I saw the supervisor she was ruffling through some pages and appeared frustrated. Put your awareness cap on and follow the PIER™ principles. It's often about creating opportunities for yourself. Never wait for opportunities. If one doesn't appear, build one.

In this case, I began with a Plan. I identified the emotion I felt she was experiencing and followed up with an *exploratory question*. My exploratory question was simply whether she needed help. I imagine she would have been just as happy taking Farah and I on even if I didn't have the experience I had.

***

Sometimes opportunities aren't obvious or
they just aren't there...yet. You may find
yourself having to create them. By doing
so, you may just get what you're after!

***

Plan, have the right Intent, make the right first impression (your entrance and engagement) and build the Relationship – even if it's brief and preliminary. The important thing is that you *ask*. That, and that you offer some value to the person you're asking the consideration from.

It doesn't need to take long – depending on what's at stake. Imagine this: had I not stepped in with a plan, observed what was unfolding, executed my approach with the right intent, engaged, offered a solution and followed the PIER™, I would have collected tickets outside the event, never heard the speakers and never would have worked with Oprah. Was it worth trying? Hell, yeah. What about you? Follow guidepost number two more from now on, and 'Just Ask.' You'll immediately begin to reap the benefits for having done so.

What lessons can you draw from the above story?
Here are a few to consider:
- Identify opportunities; and if there are none, create them.
- Take risks and know your value.
- Offer something, even if what you have to offer is nothing more than a passion to help.
- Make your very first impression an excellent one.
- Ask for the opportunity when the time is right.
- Identify a problem or emotion and provide a solution that appeals to your negotiatee.
- Just ask, dammit!

***

Fear, lack of confidence and an absence of
know how are the very stumbling blocks
that prevent you from asking and taking
chances in the first place
***

"Courage is not the absence of fear, but rather the judgement that something is more important than fear." – Ambrose Redmoon.

What's fear got to do with it?

What does fear have to do with it? Referring to the one of the three F's I told you about earlier (Fear, Forgetfulness and Familiarity), let's take a closer look at fear. So, how does fear factor into not getting what you want in life? Well, the answer to that question differs for everyone, but I've got a pretty good idea what's going on for many hopeful negotiators out there. Some of you may be answering, "Everything!" whereas others, "Not a damn thing!" Let me explain.

For many of you, asking for what you want in *life* and in *business* can seem intimidating and downright scary as hell. I mean, what if they say 'No'?! Wouldn't that just crush you?? NO, it wouldn't!! You'd live. But… what if you didn't get what you were after? Wouldn't that just discourage you from ever trying again? Again, 'NO, dammit, it mustn't!'

Is a richer, more satisfying life what you're after? If you answered 'Yes' to that, then fear should immediately be considered a foul four letter word you never use as an excuse not to ask or negotiate, with anyone, for anything, ever, *ever* again. Fear is for losers, and you're not a loser. You can't afford to be in this day and age where you're being punished for living in a time where purchasing a house for first time buyers is so freakin' out of reach, where student debt is often student death, where jobs are no longer secure and come with an expiration date and no benefits, where getting what you want often feels impossible, where your boss pushes you to seal the deal no matter what, and la-de-dah. It goes on forever. Fear must be defeated by the warrior within you, and I'll cover how to lock that evil bastard in a dungeon as you read on.

Now, for others, asking and negotiating is not intimidating, nor is it scary at all. Fear is non-existent to them. It's something they chose to get past by beating the crap out of it whenever it showed its ugly face, locking it in its dungeon where it belonged, and they took control of their lives and their destinies by keeping it from interfering with their actions. They're the ones we see with the big houses, fancy cars, great jobs and dynamite life partners. They're the ones getting more out of life, unafraid to use their **ASS**ets and create the very lives they want and deserve. They're not afraid to ask and go for what they want; and they know how to go about getting it in a suave, savvy, confident way. Shouldn't you be one of them?

No matter where you stand on this scale of fear or failure at the moment, I'd like you to remember something, right now: Asking is one of the most indispensable rights we have as humans. Yes, you read that correctly. It's a **right**. Yours and mine. This 'right' – *our* right to ask for what we want and deserve is so sadly under-utilized, it's downright sinful. So much so, that many of us seldom get what we want and deserve out of life, much to our sad misfortune and demise. We miss out on jobs, bonuses, love, and much more. Simply for not having asked or negotiated when it was our very right to do exactly that, we lost. That's got to change. It changes for you, NOW.

We all know fear. We've each experienced it at some point in our lives. Fear, lack of confidence and the lack of courage and know-how are often the very stumbling blocks that prevent us from asking in the first place, and consequently from getting what we want in life. Let's take a closer look at them.

This is an excellent place to address these agreement killers - pre-negotiation. If you suffer from any of these three agreement killers, the first two, in particular, becoming aware of it is your first step to recovery. I say recovery because both fear and lack of confidence/courage are in my opinion self-created diseases. They are the downfall of many good women and men. And they become habit if you don't actively do something to replace them with their opposites: courage and confidence.

Remaining hostage to fear and lack of self-confidence is the very essence of self-sabotage. The "know-how" you are well on your way to discovering by now. We often stick to habit - even self-sabotaging ones - because they're familiar to us and we become comfortable with familiarity, even if it's not in our best interest.

The goal is to break free from self-sabotaging familiarity to reach self-motivating familiarity. Imagine how much richer our lives would be if we dared to ask for that raise, that date, that opportunity or that deal. Imagine having the courage to leave that toxic or abusive relationship by negotiating the benefits of doing so with yourself. Imagine having no inhibitions, like your five-year-old self once experienced... Is any of this sinking in by now? I sure as heck hope so. By now, even before you've discovered the how-to, you should be feeling the want-to.

***

Replace self-sabotaging familiarity with self-motivating familiarity. That way, no matter what you do, you'll be better off.
***

Aristotle once said, "We are what we repeatedly do; excellence, then, is not an act but a habit." We must therefore strive for excellence, always.

Fear can easily become a habit preventing us from asking in the first place, especially when we allow it to settle into our thoughts and consequently our self-monologues. It can easily become far too sadly familiar to us, preventing us from exploring healthier options and taking risks. Those little voices in our heads, if permitted to be directed by fear, will prevent us from moving forward. They will keep us locked in those cages of our own making.

I'm asking you to consider breaking away from your old self-sabotaging habits of fear and reluctance (lack of confidence) and develop new empowering habits of opportunity identification, risk-taking and PIER™ negotiating. Become fearless and understand that it's your right to ask for the things that you want in life, providing you build a solid foundation for doing so first. Change your disempowering inner-monologues saturated in fear to empowering ones of fearlessness.

My daughter Cassie is an amazing example of being fearless. She oozes self-confidence. An exceptional singer and actress, she announced at the age of 12 her life's dream: she wanted to become a full-time film and stage actress. As any parent might relate, hearing this from your child congers up valid concerns, especially when you imagine how difficult it might be for your child to make a descent living at it. Can you relate to a time something similar happened to you?

Well, I supported her decision. I'd always encouraged both my daughters to go after what they wanted in life. Today she's a successful recording artist and actress in New York with her first album under her belt. Her lack of fear took her to a new land and with confidence and determination as her constant companions; and she's living a happy, fulfilled life. You have the power to do the same.

***
Confidence and determination are essential
driving forces in your pursuit to get what
you want in life.
***

Fear, rejection and your *right* to ask: working through it all

The very thing that may keep you from experiencing your first (or next) negotiation is fear and an absence of awareness that you have the right to ask for what you want, *providing* you've set the groundwork for doing so first. One of the things that often keep us from success is a fear of failure or rejection.

Fear is one of those monsters that prevents us from asking someone out, from asking for a consideration or advantage or simply for the right to be heard. Fear is so powerful that we associate pain to it. And once we associate pain to fear, we instinctively do everything within our power to avoid it. That means that we miss or avoid opportunities; and plenty of them.

That meeting you were afraid to ask for may have been granted, if only you had asked. That discount you wanted may have been given to you, if only you had asked. That help you wanted may have received, if only you'd asked. We're often too afraid to ask for things because we're afraid of being told 'No' or of being rejected altogether and/or made to feel unworthy or embarrassed, even if only in our minds. We might also find that the root cause of our fear of asking lies in our upbringing and/or environment.

Our parents once encouraged us to ask for what we wanted after all, then later instructed us to be polite and not to ask for too much. Our teachers told us to wait our turn. Whatever it was that created this fear of asking must be expunged. Fearing the *right to ask* is simply wrong and unproductive. You're worthy and entitled to ask. Pick your moments and establish the groundwork first *before* you ask. But, **just ask**.

We are very often our own worst enemies, and once those voices of self-doubt overpower our voices of encouragement and hope, we're in deep trouble. Fear keeps us hostage and prevents us from getting what we want: "What if he/she says "no"? "What if they ignore me?" "What if they reject me?" "What will people think?" We can "What if" ourselves to death, dear friends. That must end. It's time to re-program our way of dealing with this. Think, rather, "I've got an amazing chance they'll say yes!" instead.

'What ifs,' fear, the lack of confidence, joined by the absence of know-how are the very stumbling blocks that keep us from asking. When we give into them by not asking fearlessly for what we want, we may very well be visited on our deathbeds by the ghosts of missed opportunities, asking us "Why in the world did you not just ask?" When it comes to negotiating and asking, you mustn't let fear hold you back. Learn how to become fearless. Practice until you become fearless. I, for one, don't want to be visited by the ghosts of missed opportunities on my death bed reminding *me* of what I could have had if only I had asked. Do you? If you never ask, the answer will always be 'no'.

Never fear the word "No" – it's just a word, after all

I've negotiated thousands of "deals" in my career, everything from obtaining confessions from murderers to the release of hostages. One of the big mistakes negotiators consistently make is to try to get to "yes" too quickly. "No" is where most negotiations, in life and in business, begin. Hostage negotiations and interrogations all start at "no." In the business and sales worlds, I understand that many of you start at "Ground Zero," that is, with neither a 'yes' or 'no.'

'No' is not a word to be feared, it's simply a starting point. How could it be *'yes'* right away or too quickly? Be careful about the qualifier of *'yes.'* An early yes is often a trap and a trick, especially in business. It's usually followed by *"when," "if,"* or *"providing…"* Early yeses are not yeses at all. They're conditional. Those voices in your head should alert you that an early yes is wrong, without exploring it further. What we're after are sound, decision-based agreements. We don't compromise just to compromise and get the deal. We detach from the emotion of 'yes' and think rationally and carefully.

While we're on the topic of "No", I caution you about the very popular belief that 'win – win' is where everybody should strive to get to. Maybe that's why you might feel an early yes is good. I'll explain what I mean shortly.

Negotiations don't always take place in the business world as you've now discovered. The process is similar whether you're negotiating a deal or a consideration. Negotiating may feel daunting to many. But it's like everything else in life; you can learn how to do it. And you can learn how to do it well. Imagine if you were first starting to walk and decided just to give up because it was too hard. Where would you be today?

Good negotiation skills involve self-discipline: the ability to control yourself; your body language and your approach. It also involves the ability to read the body language of others sitting across from you. It involves the ability to use effective communication skills; active listening skills; self-control; self-discipline, practice; establishing your mission and purpose with your negotiatees in the forefront, your children, your parents, the shopkeeper, the bank and so forth. That's why it's important to have a valid mission statement in place, especially in business, that considers the other persons needs just as much as your own because it's by using this approach that will help you to succeed. A mission statement is a summary of your goals and intentions and I'll explore them more in depth shortly.

As I said earlier, you may feel intimidated by the negotiation process at first, but I intend to simplify things for you as we go along so that you no longer feel intimidated or fearful, which will help you move steadily towards success in just about every negotiation you undertake. Does that mean that you'll win every negotiation that you undertake? No, it doesn't. You can be equally successful knowing when to walk away from a negotiation that isn't working for you as you would be in working for the one that does.

Think of it this way: if the person you're negotiating with is asking or demanding too much of you and won't budge despite your best negotiation techniques, doesn't it make sense to know when to walk away? Sure it does. It not only saves you money in the case of a business deal, but it saves you valuable time. And is that not a win for you?

> "You cannot negotiate with people who say what's mine is mine and what's yours is negotiable"
> ~ John f. Kennedy

There are many 'sharks' out there who want nothing more than to take complete advantage of you, and they're good at what they do. Knowing your limitations and what you can and cannot live with makes you a winner just as much as sealing the deal does. Sharks – those out there who don't think twice of taking advantage of you - don't only exist in the business world but in life as well. We know they do.

Don't take a 'No' personally

No one likes to be rejected or to feel rejected. We have an overwhelming desire to feel wanted, appreciated, accepted and needed. But if you fear rejection in a negotiation or any other interaction with any another human being, you'll lose out. On the other hand, if your attitude is one of "I don't need this deal" on your way into the negotiation, how can the person sitting across from you ever possibly reject you? With that kind of mindset, it won't matter. You'll put your everything, within reason, into having your negotiatee reach a 'yes' and with that mindset, you won't be *needing* anything from them.

Can you see that by not focusing on the outcome of the negotiation it can relieve you from the stress that may very well impair your efforts? If your negotiatee has the impression that you don't need anything from them and are there simply to help them get what they want, they'll be more likely to work with you at reaching a deal that is mutually beneficial to both of you. Funny how this works.

You'll approach the interaction calmly, openly and inquisitively. That's how to do it in life as well. Don't expect a positive result from the onset because that might not happen, despite your best efforts. If you expect it, you may broadcast signals of neediness, and that will turn the other person off or have them enter the fight or flight mode. Isaac Newton's third law of motion applies nicely here. "For every action, there is an equal and opposite reaction"[12]. On the other hand, when you project confidence, are focused on the process and project a relaxed and confident attitude, you'll have a much greater chance of reaching the 'yes' you're after.

---

[12] Sir Isaac Newton was an English mathematician, astronomer, theologian, author and physicist who is widely recognized as one of the most influential scientists of all time, and a key figure in the scientific revolution.

I remember when I first became an actor auditioning for film and television. I wanted the roles I auditioned for so badly that I convinced myself I *needed* them. When I first began to audition, I'd go into the audition room with feelings of anxiety, neediness, and fear – all of which are 'agreement killers' - and they always got the better of me. The result? I wouldn't deliver the best

"Life has a way of matching you with the right role, the right deal, and the right person, if you're open to it and project the right vibrations inviting the other to reciprocate".

performance I knew I could and should have. The casting directors would sense my fear and uneasiness, and they were looking for someone who was confident, unneedy and in control of their emotions. They wanted somebody to deliver the role without having to work hard for it. That wasn't me - at first. They said 'no' more often than they said 'yes.'

Once I discovered that walking into an audition room was simply an opportunity for me to deliver my very best and to have fun with the role I was auditioning for, I started landing more roles. I no longer projected neediness, just professionalism.

Now, this didn't guarantee me that I would land every role I auditioned for; it simply meant that my chances of getting the roles were far greater. I still got rejected from time to time, but I grew not to take it personally: nor should you in any business or life negotiation. People will say 'no' for a number of different reasons. In the acting biz, it could simply mean that you didn't look like you'd fit the role. Or maybe you remind the casting director of someone they despise! Who knows? Who cares? You shouldn't. Life has a way of matching you with the right role, the right deal, and the right person, if you're open to it and project the right vibrations inviting the other to reciprocate. And if you do the work.

Saying 'No' is everybody's right

Before we move on to explore neediness a bit further, and while I'm on the topic of 'No', let me add this: we all have the right to say 'No'.

We discovered this powerful word shortly after learning how to walk. We learned to use it whenever we needed to, and it was used on us relentlessly. It often preceded our very childhoods negotiations - whether it was about bedtime, a special treat, or whatever. We've been using that word all our lives, but many of us are often fearful of using it. So afraid of hurting other people's feelings, in some cases, that we'll get hurt just to spare another's feelings. That's counterproductive.

Asserting yourself and knowing what you can and cannot live with is your responsibility. All a negotiation is, as you now understand, is a gathering between two or more people to discuss a situation that is of mutual interest to all parties, to discover whether they can reach an agreement, with all parties having the right to say "No." The more you discover how to negotiate and ask for what you want proficiently, the better off you'll be and the more comfortable you'll become using and inviting your negotiatee to use the word 'no'. It's also time to un-hostage yourself from feeling that you have no right to say "No" or that you shouldn't invite the other person to do the same.

Remember that people negotiate successfully with those they know, like and trust. What better way to get somebody to trust and respect you than to invite them to say 'no' if they're not happy with what they're hearing? You're not giving up on what matters to you. Far from it. You're inviting discussion to allow you to make a proposal later on. You'll not be projecting yourself as someone who's needy or pushy.

***
Inviting someone to say 'no' often gets
them thinking yes, because you're putting
absolutely no pressure on them. They
become more open to what you have to say
and offer.
***

No one wants to enter a relationship of any kind with someone who is needy or pushy. The word "No" is something that every serious and good negotiator should be prepared to use immediately before, during or at the conclusion of every negotiation, be it in life or in business. Sometimes saying 'no' is the best thing to say, the right thing to say, the only thing to say; and it's your right to say it.

I'm very aware that many of you are going to have a tough time getting used to the concept of leading with the word "No," or in simply using it when it begs to be used. But to become an exceptional negotiator, it's vital that you get comfortable in do so. It's important that you understand your personal worth, your company's worth, and your products' or services' worth. Once you understand the foregoing and the value attached to it, you can move forward into the negotiation confidently.

I must admit that I had a hard time doing so in the beginning. Once I'd left the police service after thirty-one years of duty and following my TEDx talk (starting my own business in the keynote speaking field) I didn't yet know my worth as a keynote speaker. I knew I was good at it and that what I had to share was of value to potential clients, but I had no clue what dollar value to attach to my services at first.

It was through the assistance of my brother Robaire, my speaking coaches, my friend Farah, as well as my own personal research on the matter that I discovered what value to attach to my services. The more I asserted my value/worth in my own mind, the easier

> **The word "No" is something that every serious and good negotiator should be prepared to use immediately before, during or at the conclusion of every negotiation.**

it became to negotiate for what I deserved, and what was fair. I began asking for what I was worth, and I was prepared to negotiate within reason to get it, always. By being confident in my own worth, those I negotiated with were also confident in my worth.

I remember being contacted by a highly successful company in Paris, France, who wanted to secure my keynote speaking services on how to successfully negotiate in business for a half-day seminar they were planning in Lisbon, Portugal. As you can imagine, I was extremely interested in providing them with the principles of the negotiation process, and the fact that it involved a trip to Portugal made it that much sweeter! But instead of providing them with a quote for my services, I responded to their initial e-mail inquiry by asking what their budget was. To my surprise, it was almost twice as much as I would have asked originally. And it was fair as it turns out.

I was at that stage just beginning to realize my services' worth. Had I not asked what their budget was, I would have asked for much less, and this might have caused them concern. How? A good product costs a fair dollar – a bad one, not so much. They might have imagined 'he's not good enough.' That experience taught me a valuable lesson: don't undervalue yourself no matter if it's business or personal. And in this case, is this one of those rare instances where you reach an agreement of "yes" right from the onset? It is, in part. There are other considerations in a negotiation. I then proceeded to negotiate transportation and accommodation, which had not been clarified in their original proposal.

Be honest and upfront, and know how and when to use the word 'No'

The word "No" is not irreversible. It is reversible. Don't be afraid of telling your negotiatee that you're perfectly fine hearing the word "No." This applies primarily to business negotiations and acts to relax your negotiatee. That's also being honest, as much as you may think that using this approach is counterproductive. This approach helps establish trust and rapport, and makes the person sitting across from you that much more comfortable and at ease. As the negotiation progresses, you'll then provide your negotiatee with incentives to see the value in what you're offering to reach a 'yes.'

No matter how hard-nosed a negotiator they may be, being upfront, honest and direct will help build trust between the two of you. If it doesn't, walk. Don't waste your precious time. When you become comfortable enough using the word 'No' and begin to use it calculatedly, your negotiatee will relax, the trust between the two of you will heighten, and that long-term professional relationship you were looking for will develop naturally.

In your world, if there's something that you can't deliver on, just say so. Don't beat around the bush or make shit up. Use a low, calm, controlled voice (a late-night radio hosts' voice, for example) and say so. Project a confident and controlled tone of voice, and move on, or suggest an alternative. In hostage negotiations, for example, some requests were simply impossible to consider. Replying, "John, that's just not possible. How do you expect me to do that?" works.

Again, the voice tone and projection are low, calm, non-threatening and simply state fact. If you can't deliver something they need, consider referring them to someone who can.

Make the right impression, believe that the product and/or service that you're offering is right for your negotiatee (even when that 'product' is you!), *listen* to them and *ask* questions. Be open-minded. Remain mindful that you explore thoroughly with the intent of finding the best

> **Whenever possible get to the heart of the matter by taking the time to explore what the heart of the matter is.**

solutions for their needs and concerns; by doing so, not only will you have done your job, but you will also have done it well. Use your voice and body language to project sincerity. That approach will considerably enhance the possibility of *not only* closing the deal but may lead to a partnership that will foster repeat business and/or much-appreciated referrals. And that's what a successful negotiation is: getting what you want while considering the needs, wants and expectations of the other to give them what they want.

In negotiations and the skillful art of asking, you want a mindset of discovery and must become an accomplished communicator and listener to extract information important to the overall outcome. Plan for the expected and the unexpected and have your answers ready. Never assume. It's ok if later you're thrown a question you didn't expect, because by then you will have established enough rapport and trust to assure your client or prospect that you will get that answer for them forthwith. We just never know what's going to be thrown at us; but the more we prepare, the more likely we are to have the answers when the concerns or questions come up.

Internal and external factors: controlling one to influence the other

Before you negotiate, be aware that there are both internal and external factors at play in each negotiation. This applies to every negotiation. We can control the internal factors as they exist within ourselves; they are our moods, our words and our body gestures. But we can't control external factors, as they are NOT within ourselves – but in others. So, in controlling ourselves, the key is to be upfront, authentic, truthful and prepared. Say what you mean and mean what you say.

Whenever possible get to the heart of the matter by taking the time to explore what the heart of the matter is. Increase your awareness of what's developing throughout. Prepare yourself mentally to behave humanely, fairly and genuinely. This is what I call **intent,** which I'll explore in greater detail in one of the next chapters.

As you prepare, consider what success might look like to *your* negotiatee. Later, 'just ask' what it means to them. Never guess what your client or negotiatee needs or what he or she sees as success for them. You've gotta ask them.

Think of what we do when we first meet or start chatting with a potential partner. We slowly explore what they're looking for: what 'success' (their ideal partner) looks like to them. We discover their likes and dislikes. We get to know them as they get to know us. We create likeability, if we're interested in them. I know I use 'dating' as a business and life comparison, but I do so simply because they are so freakin' similar. It's a courtship after all, not unlike many of our day-to-day and business experiences.

Become as fearless and confident as possible; be flexible and inquisitive; have fun in discovering how you can meet your negotiatees' needs. Isn't that the best way to score a date? It works in business just as well. JUST ASK. I assure you that despite whatever level of confidence you may have at this moment, once you deploy the principles of what you're discovering here, that lack of confidence will be replaced by confidence and courage, and you'll become extremely comfortable with the process of how to negotiate or ask. When that happens, you'll navigate through it all easily and exceptionally well.

As a hostage negotiator, I could never guess what the hostage-taker or person in crisis was going through or whatever invisible noose they had around their neck. I had to ask them what they were going through, how they were feeling and what I could do to help. It astounds the heck out of me that in the business world so many business people try to guess what their negotiatee needs and propose something to them without gathering all the facts. That makes no sense whatsoever. Don't fall into that dumbass way of getting what you're after. Far too many business negotiators guess what their client wants or whether they're even in the position of affording what they're after.

Here's another story. This one from my professional career as a cop, and it deals with stressors and worries our negotiatee's may be experiencing even before we come into the picture. It's important to consider what worries your negotiatee might be experiencing because your job will be to un-worry them as much as possible and set them at ease enough to listen to you. It will require asking questions and getting to the heart of their fears or reluctance, should either exist.

I remember my very *first* crisis negotiation. I was patrol sergeant and was called to a residence for an unknown 9-1-1 disturbance. When I got to the place, I discovered the front door to the residence was slightly ajar, and I knocked cautiously. I was the first responder to arrive at the scene, and after opening the door a tad further, I called out and identified myself as a police officer. I asked if everyone inside was okay. I then heard a voice beckoning me up a staircase, and I moved cautiously towards the sound of the voice, not knowing if I was going to be ambushed or exactly what the hell I was getting into.

When I got to the bottom of the stairs and began to move cautiously upward, with my hand on my service revolver holster just in case, I saw the frame of a metal chair at the top of the landing above of me. I had no idea what I was walking into, but I knew someone was up there summoning me to come closer. Then I saw feet. A man was recklessly trying to balance himself on a flimsy metal framed chair, and to make matters even worse, the seat was missing from the chair. All I could see at that point were this guy's feet sliding on this fragile framed, seat-less chair. One step closer and I could see him in his entirety now. He was standing on the flimsy chair with a thick rope noose around his neck. And he was piss ass drunk.

In one hand he was holding a half bottle of Jack Daniel's, and in his other, he had an open-bladed, razor sharp box cutter. Drunk as a skunk. I now knew I was dealing with a suicidal man who was high to boot. He was swaying back and forth; his speech was slurred, and his eyes were glazed and unfocused. "Good. You're here. I want you to witness my suicide, so you can tell my effing wife just how I went out", is all he managed to slur out at first.

This depressed soul was clearly in a very dangerous state, in mind and in body, and he was looking to me for closure or as the witness to his very last, sad breath. I knew that in my first few seconds with him I was going to have to establish a meaningful, positive impression on him if I was going to succeed in gaining his trust and later, his cooperation.

I also knew that one false move and he'd fall or jump off the chair, the noose would tighten around his neck or even snap it like a dry twig, and I wouldn't be able to rush up and lift him to relieve the pressure without placing myself in immediate and lethal danger. His body would be flailing violently, and the razor-sharp box cutter in his right hand would cut through me like a samurai's sword blade slicing through soft butter. I'd be dead or critically injured within seconds. I knew that I had to change his state and his way of seeing things if I were to get him down safely.

To get what I wanted (him down safely) I had to give him something he wanted. Sometimes that's as simple as giving someone an ear so they can vent. I also wanted to provide him with a solution of some kind that he not only could 'live with', but would be happy to. I couldn't make it all about me – barking some damn cop commands that he get off the chair 'or else'. Yeah, like that would work. What am I going to do, threaten to shoot him? Don't get me started. Anyway, I also had to get him to see me not as a cop or his adversary, or in this case, as simply a witness to his suicide. No. I had to get him to trust me; and I had to get him to listen to me. Fast. That meant getting him to talk and tell me what he wanted and needed. I had to understand his circumstances from his point of view before I could offer my two cents. That's the way it works when you're after something. You gotta let them talk and tell first. You gotta see it through their eyes.

***

Understanding your negotiatee's point of
view before sharing your own is an
important step in any successful negotiation
or ask.

***

In this case, I used my first few seconds very calculatedly, and in a controlled, non-threatening voice – my midnight radio broadcasters voice, I began. With open hands, palms up, I introduced myself this time by using my first name and assured him I was there to help him. "My name is Paul. You look like you're having a really bad day. I have no idea what you're going through, but I'd like to hear what's going on. Tell me. I can help." I asked him for his name and got him talking about what he was going through – his problems and what got him to this breaking point. The dynamics slowly moved from him being in complete control (he was calling all the shots at first, right? It was his show and I was merely a spectator at first) to my eventual taking of control, accomplishing this through carefully chosen words, tone of voice, body language, empathy, rapport and *exploratory dialogue*[13].

I got him to talk and vent his frustrations out and I asked a lot of questions prompting him to imagine his own solutions. Eventually, I earned the right to offer my own solutions and 'proposals' to him, but only once I understood where *he* was coming from. Giving him an opportunity to 'let it all out' provided me important information as well as an opportunity to bond and negotiate further, since I now understood what led him to this crisis in the first place.

You might be wondering what my cop story about a man with a noose around his neck has to do with *your* world of asking and negotiating. I asked you to think of your own circumstances as you read my stories, to keep an open mind, so can you see it? If I stop here to look at *your world* for a moment, I'm quite certain that you're not going to be walking into an office building or any other place to negotiate or discuss a deal with a man or woman who has a physical noose around their neck – unless you're a hostage or crisis negotiator that is. However, for many of you, you may often be

---

[13] Much more on this later

walking into a situation where you don't have all the facts and you'll have no idea what's really going on in the mind of your negotiatee(s), or what solutions they're looking to get. They may be going through their own personal nightmares and dealing with their own business or personal circumstances – their invisible nooses, shall we say. A noose is exactly that: a stress, concern, worry, fear or whatever that impedes rational thinking or creates a wall. We all have them at some point. They choke the life out of us.

Think business negotiations or even a job interview. As may be often the case, that noose - or a noose – may be there, but it will be under the disguise of something quite different from the one I encountered in my 'man with the noose' story. It may be that they just dealt with a company that didn't deliver on their promises, a life partner who messed them up, or a multitude of other stressors. Consider this as you enter your next negotiation. Don't neglect examining whatever noose you might be wearing yourself which may be preventing you from focusing on what really matters and giving it your absolute best. If you don't get rid of your nooses, you'll choke. If you don't get rid of their nooses, they'll choke. I'll help you understand how to remove the nooses: yours and theirs.

No, not everyone is going to see you as the enemy either; of course not. But many of your negotiatee's will have their own invisible 'nooses', be it budget cuts, other offers to consider, former employees that let them down, or whatever - it will be your job to identify and remove their nooses in order to establish trust and cooperation, granting you the opportunity to take the negotiation further. You earn the right to ask and negotiate once you know what they're after and once there are no nooses left to remove. Till then, you're simply taking blind shots praying something will get into the net.

In the scenario I've just provided, it only took thirty minutes for me to talk this poor soul down to safety using the PIER™ Principles you're about to discover within the pages of this book. I provided him a solution he was willing to 'live' with. His noose was then physically and somewhat emotionally removed. That happened because I encouraged him to tell me what led him to his state of crisis, providing him with the right to be heard and validated throughout. It happened because I asked questions, explored his world in depth, showed empathy and didn't push. It's when this occurs that trust and lasting agreements of value can develop and prosper.

Business bulletin # 3:

Ask what the client wants, how important it is for them in finding a solution, how much they're willing to spend in finding that solution, as well as what their fears are. Ask them if they've been talking with someone else or whether they're talking to someone else right now. That's all part of exploratory dialogue. Never guess, assume or avoid. Your job is to *identify and ask.*

Now let's move on to *need*. I labored on exactly where to insert this important piece and it makes complete sense to insert it here, before we delve further into the PIER™.

Neediness

To further examine the neediness anomaly I touched upon earlier, neediness (rather, a specific kind of neediness) must be completely exterminated before ever entering any negotiation, be it in life or in business.

This should not be confused with 'legitimate neediness', a topic I'll get to further on. What I'm referring to here is 'ugly' neediness - that sense that you need this deal or other emotional thing to happen,

79

at whatever cost. Because, most often, you simply don't. That's weakness, and will be seen as such, because you'll not be able to hide that kind of neediness. It will show in either your body language, your words, your tone of voice, your actions, or each of these broadcasters. It will seep out from each of your pores and your negotiatee will see all its ugliness for what it is. And they'll run.

What do we actually "need" in this world? Do we "need" the latest smartphone, new car, new pair of shoes? No, if we're to be truthful with ourselves, we don't "need" them - not in the life-and-death sense. We'd like them. There's a big difference.

What we need are the essentials of life to survive: food, water, shelter, oxygen, companionship, love and that which keeps us alive and motivated to live another day. We don't "need" any deal we may be after – or whatever else we may be looking to get from your life and business negotiations. It would be nice to get what you're after, but most often, we don't need it. We want it. Understanding the difference between needing and wanting will help us get what we're after. Does that sound ridiculous? By not needing it, you'll have a better chance of getting it.

Now I'm not suggesting that there are legitimate needs a client/negotiatee may have that must be fulfilled as I earlier eluded to. The 'need' I'm referring to in this passage is that ugly 'neediness.' The begging, pleading, "I can't live without it/without you," kind of neediness. You must be equals at the negotiation table.

In the context of being 'equals' at the negotiation table, should neediness pop up in one of the negotiators, the underdog becomes the person without the 'ugly' needs. The needy one becomes the slave to the negotiation. He/she must work harder, and the chances of reward are not as great. As previously discussed, if you "want" the deal (or whatever you've set out to get) but don't need it, you're more likely to behave more casually, professionally and comfortably, and work effortlessly at reaching solutions that work for both of you, and that will help you immensely in achieving it.

In business, your negotiatee may be a competitor; and, like yourself, they are constantly evaluating you and how the negotiation is unfolding, making determinations on what they see and hear and how they're feeling about the process. If they sense neediness in you, they'll consider that as a sign of weakness or greed and act accordingly. Neither of these will make you look good and can easily kill the deal or leave you open to be taken advantage of.

Your body language, the tone of your voice, the words you use and so much more will give that neediness in you away. Words account for less than 10% of what you're communicating. The rest is broadcasted through body language and the tone and pitch of your voice. If you project neediness in the negotiation, you'll be regarded as desperate… and who wants to deal with a desperate person? You never want to project neediness in a business relationship or in a personal relationship. Or with a loans officer, a prospective boss or a million and one other potential opportunities, for that matter.

Never guess, assume or avoid. Your job is to identify and ask.

It doesn't matter what you're negotiating for in life or in business, but when you project neediness, people tend to back away from you and put their guards up. It's unattractive. It could be as simple as a young man asking a young woman out for a date. If he projects neediness in his approach, she's not likely to fall for him or to agree to a date. What she's after is someone who is confident and capable, someone strong that she can trust, and someone who has given her a solid reason to say 'yes.' The same is true in business. As a good negotiator aspiring to be excellent, you must never be needy.

***
Neediness, to the point of being desperate,
will open you to being used, and perhaps
even abused. It certainly won't get you
what you deserve. Never be ugly-needy.
That's just unattractive and counterproductive.
***

The 'no neediness' zone

Let's shift focus for a moment and examine 'worth' in the context of neediness: yours and theirs. Being equal in the negotiation and when meeting anyone you hope to be collaborating with is vitally crucial. It sets a professional tone between each of you. Understanding your worth helps level the playing field. Whether inside or outside the business world, being equal sets a personal, welcomed, non-intimidating tone. No one should be the top dog in any room, no one better than the other. You both walk in with your wants (and legitimate needs) and if one of the negotiators is out of balance, the one projecting neediness, for example, the other will pick up on it, and suddenly the power dynamic changes and you are no longer equals.

Begging and pleading have no place at any negotiation, be it in life or in business

One of my earliest recollections of any semblance of a negotiation was when I was around ten years old, 'negotiating' with my mom to get her to intervene on my behalf with my father, who every Saturday morning, insisted on giving me and my younger brother a buzz cut. Alright, I'll admit, it wasn't a negotiation as much as it was me begging and pleading to be excused from that dreaded haircut. It was the mid-sixties, and the Beatles had arrived in North

America, bringing along with them new and wonderful hairstyles for men. Buzz cuts were dead – but not in the Nadeau household. I lost that negotiation with mom. Every time. She didn't want to poke the already angry bear. I understand that now.

I discovered on my journey through life that begging and pleading (displaying neediness) is not the way to negotiate and get what you want. You may be laughing right now thinking, 'who does that?' You'd be surprised. Many adults have modified begging and pleading to showing neediness. There's no difference: it's the same thing.

As for me, I went from begging and pleading to building trust, likeability and strong interpersonal relationships with my clients. I found that approach to be much more successful than begging and pleading. I also knew when to walk away. As should you. Nobody wants to deal with a weak, emotionally needy individual. It's imperative to know what you want and go after what you want, yes, but don't get so emotionally attached to that want to think you need it. Know when to *stop* asking before the label 'needy' is affixed to you in the mind of the client or individual you're dealing with.

PART 3

LISTEN WITH YOUR SOUL

Guidepost number three: Listen *with your soul*

Listen with your soul. You may have caught me using this expression earlier. It's time for me to explain what I mean by this. To listen with your soul is to listen with your ears, your eyes, your body **and** your heart. Full-bodied listening, baby! Listen with the intent of truly understanding the other person and their point of view, no matter how unique or different it may be from yours.

Don't engage in the act of partial listening, when all you want to do is tell the other person what you think without first actively and *soulfully* listening to them. Let go of your ego and what you're after at first. Leave that ego at the door, always - it has no place in negotiation, soul listening and asking, for that matter.

It's my absolute belief that if we listened to others with our souls, we could quite possibly solve many of the world's volatile problems. We could very well end wars and build bridges of understanding and cooperation instead of impenetrable walls and roadblocks. Imagine listening to one another with the intent of understanding them first, and then working on agreements and solutions of mutual benefit as opposed to forcing our ideas on another or dismissing theirs altogether. Think of our current crisis' around the globe. Did forcing opinions and beliefs on others work in those instances? Will building walls really make things better?

Soul listening includes being genuinely empathetic and open to the other. No matter what the other person says, be genuine with your intent in trying to understand their point of view. You don't necessarily have to agree – no, of course not. But you do have to refrain from judging and from accusation. We're more similar than we are different, and it's imperative for us to remember that there are distinct differences, yes, and those differences are largely founded on nature, nurture and experience. They're a result of environment, upbringing, what we were taught to believe and what we chose/choose to believe.

When you listen with your soul, you won't judge. You won't accuse. You'll make a sincere effort to understand the point of view of the one you're engaging with. You'll value the differences as their right to think differently. You won't *listen* while thinking of your next statement. That's not listening at all. Soul listening builds rapport and makes the other feel important and acknowledged.

> To listen with your soul is to listen with your ears, your eyes, your body and your heart. Listen with the intent of truly understanding the other person and their point of view, no matter how unique or different it may be from yours.

It lowers whatever bridge or defense they may have, offering you an opportunity to move forward. This is an essential key to successful negotiating. It does not mean you'll always agree. It simply means you'll listen with a genuine intent to understand and work from there.

You have two ears – there's a reason for that

Listen instead of talking. Of course, you're going to talk and present your point of view as well as propose a solution when the time is right – but don't be surprised if it changes once you've heard from your negotiatee.

Being open-minded can take you to much better places you'd never imagined. Rid yourself of the belief that you "need" to talk first or get everything out in the first few minutes of any negotiation. You don't have to impress anyone right from the very beginning with your credentials or imaginary solutions, without first discovering the facts at play.

Once connection and purpose have been established, begin by creating rapport and setting the stage for the negotiation to follow. In a planned negotiation, begin with a pleasant conversation to warm things up, and the actual 'negotiation' will come later once that conversation leads to exploratory dialogue and you grasp their point of view. Make your questions fit the negotiation. Ask the right questions to get the most out of the exchange.

I don't want you to get hung up on the conversation aspect of the negotiation just yet. I'll explore that later. I'm not suggesting for a moment that the initial conversation must be ten or fifteen minutes long. You'll know when to get on with the actual negotiation, but I want you to appreciate and enjoy a conversation before you do, because it helps establish that all-important rapport. Be genuinely interested in your negotiatee and their wants.

Once you've had that conversation, you'll have earned the right to move ahead to the discussion and eventually ask for what you want.

Negotiations are largely about building relationships. They're about active listening, paraphrasing, mirroring, meeting needs on both sides and not compromising to anyone's detriment. Remember, using the "I don't need this deal" mentality will help reach an agreement that you're both willing and happy to accept. That applies to life negotiations just as equally. It sends out relaxed and confident vibrations, and not ones of uncertainty or neediness.

Now in the case of a hostage negotiation, there can be no *conversation* to build rapport at the onset, because of the immediate urgency to get the job done. In cases such as these, where the unexpected negotiation arises or some other urgency, talking about the weather or what you may have in common isn't what's called for. There will be times you'll need to get right down to freakin' business, take control and lead with a proposition, building the conversation as you go along. Choose your moments based on the circumstances and the urgency of the situation. Let your words and actions fit the negotiation.

***

Listening is perhaps one of the best ways to establish rapport. Soul listening involves your entire body... and your heart.

***

Contrary to what many people might believe, listening is not a passive action at all. It's an active exercise. Negotiations are about reaching agreements – together, and *that* can only be achieved if you listen soulfully. The one who *wants* the most in the negotiation is the one who ought to do most of the listening. Simply put, soul listening is one of the most important aspects of the communication skills that a negotiator must not only understand but must know how to use skillfully.

The varying skills of soul listening include using open-ended, meaningful questions; identifying emotion; mirroring/reflecting; using silence; paraphrasing what the other has said and summarizing what you've understood the other to say. These skills must all come in to play. Soul listening allows the negotiator to collect vital information from the other person (in business negotiations this is called 'discovering the interests behind the positions,' whereas I call it 'exploratory dialogue' for all our negotiations) while it's also equally important to demonstrate empathy, compassion, and rapport while doing so.

One of the biggest problems that continually shows up in ineffective communication is that we prepare our next statement while the other person is still speaking, as opposed to listening soulfully to him/her, thus only hearing what we're preparing to say in our own minds. We simply

One of the biggest problems that continually shows up in ineffective communication is that we prepare our next statement while the other person is still speaking

don't listen or do so with such ineffectiveness we only catch part of what is being said. As such, we often miss the content and emotion behind what is being said. We miss 'watching' for all-important facial expressions, shifts in posture tone changes – all of which are being broadcasted to the receiver for dissection. All of which is part of the overall message.

If you're doing the same in your day-to-day negotiations or with your family and loved ones, stop it now. Right now. You've read enough already to know you won't get the best out of an interaction, an ask or a negotiation if you lead first, don't listen and make it all about you.

In crisis negotiations, soul listening is vitally important because it allows the person in crisis to talk – to process their experience, providing the negotiator an understanding of what led them to crisis (consider my 'man in the noose' story). Additionally, the negotiatee 'sees' you're listening. It registers in their brain and they feel validated. It's the same in any negotiation. Granted, I understand that you may not be dealing with a crisis very often, but there is a reason we listen first and encourage the other to open up.

By listening to the other person lay it all out for you while you soulfully listen and provide small encouragers like "yes," "uh-huh" and "go on," you not only collect vital information, you give your negotiatee the impression you care about them enough to listen. The same is true when you're lending an ear to a loved one who simply needs to vent.

Think about the last time you felt yourself in crisis or even a bit down or depressed: did you want to *talk* or *listen* to the other person first? If you're anything like me (and I know you are – we are more similar than we are different, after all) at first you wanted - *and needed* - to talk about what you are experiencing – to be heard and understood.

After you'd 'vented' you were more inclined to invite the other to speak and share their thoughts. You felt validated and heard then – and maybe even a bit exhausted, but in a good way - and having been partnered with a good listener, you may have even discovered the solution to your crisis on your own or with gentle guidance from them; simply by venting and letting it all out. And by being a good listener in return. You may have even thanked the other person for having helped – and if they were listening with their soul, they did, when you think about it.

With that in mind, by soulfully listening to your negotiatee talk and by providing brief encouragers, you're demonstrating that you're interested, invested and there to help. It lets your negotiatee know that he/she is being heard. Soul listening reduces the negative or defensive emotions the other may be harboring.

Use short verbal cues and encouragers such as, "Uh-huh," "yes" and "I understand" along with nodding and occasionally leaning in or mirroring their posture when appropriate, and these simple motivators will usually prompt the other person to continue talking.

Try using one or a very few words of their last statement to prompt even more information. For example, if your negotiatee tells you "and that made me upset," reply with "that made you upset?" with a slight tone of inquisitiveness in your voice. They'll naturally respond to this and add more information[14]. These prompts acknowledge to the other individual that you've been listening, and they encourage the disclosure of more vital information.

Without soul listening, you may as well just talk and talk – nobody's going to listen anyway

The key to soul listening effectiveness is to coordinate the skills of listening, understanding, paraphrasing, observing body language and engaging in open dialogue. Use these skills strategically - and if you *have* been soulfully listening, you'll be equipped to ask for more information as the opportunities to do so arise. And your negotiatee will be more at ease to provide what you're after.

If during your negotiation you strike a nerve and they suddenly looked pissed, worried or in shock, try labelling the emotion you sense has just arisen. Don't ignore it. Ignoring an emotion is the wrong thing to do and it is a common mistake many negotiators make, no matter the circumstances.

Business bulletin # 4: Acknowledge the elephant.

If you're engaged in a business negotiation and what you've just said seems to have concerned your potential client, use an emotional label to identify and explore the emotion. I call it 'confronting the (white) elephant', which I'll get into in more depth later.

---

[14] I'll provide you more on this later

One of the biggest problems that continually shows up in ineffective communication is that we prepare our next statement while the other person is still speaking, as opposed to listening actively to him/her, thus only focusing on what we're preparing to say next.

An emotional label is identifying what emotion you sense the other is going through and saying so. If you sense the client became concerned with what you just said, you should slow things down to focus on what just happened. You won't ignore the barrier that just arose.

Use an open-ended question, such as: "John, you sound concerned by what I just said. Tell me…what are your thoughts about this right now?" before moving on. Notice I just used a *command* statement, and not a request? "Tell me" prompts a direct answer, whereas "Would you tell me?" does not. Identifying the emotion and then attaching an emotional label (i.e., fear, anger, confusion, etc.) to the emotion you've identified informs the person that you understand their emotion; and the open-ended question (or soft demand) invites them to continue talking and answer you[15].

The same is true if you're interacting or negotiating with your child, parent, partner or anyone else. Label what you sense they're experiencing. They may correct you, but that's considered a win. It shows them you care. Never ignore any valid emotion that creeps into a negotiation, be it in life or in business. If you sense it, feel it or hear it, you must *explore* it at the very first opportunity. Break away from the flow of the negotiation or inquiry and address the emotion then and there. Later you can proceed as planned.

---

[15] More on the topic of labelling emotion to follow

This works in your personal relationships as much as it does in your professional ones. Imagine an exchange with your significant other, and you suddenly sense they've become upset by something that you've just said. It would be a mistake to continue talking without addressing that emotion first. It would also be a mistake to repeat what you've just said or speed up the conversation in an effort to convince your significant other that you're right or that you just ignored the emotion that crept in. That wouldn't be 'soul listening,' now would it? No, the best way to handle a situation like that is to slow down, pause, identify the emotion and ask for clarification: "Honey, I sense that what I just said upset you…" Invite a reply.

Clarification eliminates guessing and making ASSumptions that may be wrong

If you're not clear about something, don't assume to understand. Instead, ask if you're right. Try something like, "If I understand you correctly, what you're saying is…" and repeat what it is that you believe to have understood. This invites you negotiatee to confirm or clarify what it is that was just said. This approach will impress your negotiatee because they'll feel that you're making every effort to understand their position. Never be embarrassed, shy or afraid of admitting you don't understand. To neglect asking for clarification when clarification is required sets you up to make false assumptions and may screw up the whole deal as well as jeopardize the relationship. You may very well end up looking like an ass to your negotiatee, and that's definitely not what you want to look like to them.

Let's go back to when I asked you to imagine the last time you felt in crisis, down or depressed. If the person you had spoken to treated you the way I've outlined so far – by listening to you with their soul, encouraged you to lay it all out, connected with what you said non-judgmentally, would that not have helped? It certainly would have.

Just feeling that the other person cares enough to listen and encourage you to open up often helps you reach your objectives and solutions. It helps to be a soul listener. As I said, this works in business as well as in your personal life. Think personal relationships and conflict resolution. How much better off are you by listening to the other person first with the intent of truly discovering their point of view? The answer is: a shit load better.

Life is too complex to follow a static script of any kind

I'll begin addressing scripts by saying that I believe scripts have a place, but not in negotiations. Negotiations are far too complex to stick to a script. Rarely will there ever be exceptions.

Following a strict, static script in the negotiations' world will leave you narrow-minded and suffering from tunnel vision. You'll focus on the order of the script before you and miss out on being authentic. You're likely to miss the bigger picture of what's really going on with your negotiatee and miss how much more you might explore, offer and accomplish to bring about the very best outcome when flexibility figures into the equation of your approach. Scripts don't leave much room, if any, for being flexible and open minded.

If you're focused exclusively on your end goal and following a script to get you there, the script you have for achieving that goal will allow you very little opportunity to be *present in the moment* and take advantage of opportunities which arise for connection and discussion. You may miss countless opportunities for successful results because your eyes will not see, your ears will not hear, and your mind will not be in negotiatee-based mode. Subtle nuances, fluctuations in your negotiatees voice, a shift in their body language, an emotion that pops into the negotiation will all be lost because you'll be following an outdated negotiators' or static sales/business script.

In the world of policing, we've discovered a great deal over the years and have made monumental progress. This involved breaking away from hard scripts and former patterns of reaction which allowed little to no room to negotiate or involve the negotiatee in reaching solutions. Whether a written script or not, that hardened way of doing things because "that's just the way we've always done it" had to change. Policing was far overdue for client-focused negotiating. Arguably, not all police officers have evolved to adopt a negotiatee/client-first mentality; but for those who have, they've achieved a much greater degree of success and cooperation.

Police are historically known to *demand* order and cooperation first and not *ask* or *negotiate* for it. Just as former day hostage negotiators did. That approach has been used for far too long; and sadly, some police still stand by that outdated and destructive code. It's changing to a degree – as it must, but not fast enough.

I admit that in law enforcement there are times where immediate action must absolutely be taken as there is no opportunity to ask or negotiate. This applies to life and business as equally as I eluded to earlier when I mentioned that at times you won't be able to work on rapport building at first. You'll just have to get right down to the nitty gritty of it, roll your sleeves up and do what has to be done, building conversation and rapport when the situation permits it. Those are the exceptions to the application of negotiation.

But just as hostage negotiations evolved, so must the *police approach* evolve, and so must all negotiations evolve, yours included. We should no longer approach our negotiations with a "who has the upper hand or the most bargaining power" mentality, nor should we stick to a script that allows little deviation from. Like

I said, the new negotiators and entrepreneurs are embracing the relationship approach to getting what they're after and so must you.

Remember: Negotiations are dynamic and unpredictable, and the individual or individuals you deal with in any of your negotiations deserve to be heard, understood and acknowledged *before* you propose a solution. Following a script will not allow you to reap the benefits of involving your negotiatee in reaching the best solutions together.

***

Unless you're an actor, kill the script...

***

Business Bulletin # 5: Kill the script

I'd like this next passage to clarify precisely what I mean by 'following a script' as opposed to being prepared to answer what may undoubtedly come up. There's a big difference. I'm very much against following a strict script – unless it's absolutely necessary *and* it doesn't sound as though it's been memorized, delivered with a lack of life and zest, or read from your desk - dead in its ability to sound natural, intriguing and real.

How many of you just hate, and I mean *hate,* when you're on the phone with a bank or a cell phone service provider for example, and they begin reading their pitch for a service you may or may not be interested in - their *script* - as opposed to simply engaging naturally with you in conversation and dialogue? I don't know about you, but it drives me absolutely stupid. I can't wait for them to be done, so much so I often interrupt with a "Dude, dude. I'm not interested." I would much prefer the human on the other end of the line to sound genuinely interested in me and what may appeal to me and say something like, "Hey Paul, I don't know if this offer I have is of any interest to you, I just don't know, but have you heard about...?"

Talking to me in that way, casually, conversationally, and with a pleasant tone of inquisitiveness is far more effective than reading an insincere script. The delivery would then sound like a natural, pleasant conversation between two people, one of whom is genuinely interested in knowing if the deal they have to offer might be of particular interest to the other.

Now I understand that some businesses won't permit their employees to go *off script;* and on that point, I'll simply say this (and you can use this in any negotiation): make it authentic. If you must follow a script, memorize it until it becomes so natural to you that nobody will know that you're using one. Just like the reference I made about actors. You know bad acting when you see and hear it. Make it sound like you killed the script.

Remember that you're not talking to an unemotional blob. You're talking to an emotional, reactive individual being, and if you sound like you're reading something, that individual will get turned off. They'll feel that you're simply trying to pitch them something without considering what they may really need, and they'll shut down and tune you out faster than you can reach the first word of the second line. It's like when someone starts screaming at you - you tend not to listen and tune them out from that point on.

Negotiating and asking for what you want should never involve bland, lifeless scripts

A negotiation should never be a scripted assortment of self-serving words that, should your negotiatee respond in one way, you automatically go to the next line in the script; and if that one doesn't work, you go to the next scripted line, and so on. That's ineffective and has limitations. Negotiations are too dynamic for that approach. Using that method *proves* that you are <u>not</u> listening to the other individual at all, and they'll pick up on it.

There's so much more to successful negotiations than following a script. Prepare and strategize, yes. But don't script it out to the point where a slight deviation will have you scrambling for what to say next. Preparing answers to potential questions that may be asked is different however. You'll never know what you may be asked, but by preparing for what might be asked, you'll be ready to informatively answer their queries.

Now let's look at some of the lessons I'd like you to *take away* from this first chapter.

Foundation - Key Points:

- No manipulating. You won't need to in order to get what you want in life.

- People respond much better when they are understood and given a chance to be heard first, and not when they are told what to do or how to feel.

- Everyone has an inherent need to be heard and validated. Considering the other person's needs and wants helps you connect and ultimately influences the outcome more positively.

- The 'You listen to me first' approach to negotiations and human interaction builds walls and *not* bridges.

- Successful negotiations are about connecting with the person across from you, listening, being open to their ideas, establishing trust and rapport and expressing solutions once you completely understand their needs, concerns, and desires.

- Listening is one of the most effective ways of establishing connection. Adopt a 20/80% rule. Do 20% of the talking and 80% of the listening. This applies to relationships involving your loved ones, a date, a business meeting and so forth.

- Ugly neediness is weakness and will be seen as such, because we will not be able to hide that neediness. As adults, the begging and pleading of our childhoods has manifested itself into neediness: an ugly frailty in the human experience.

- A negotiation is not a scripted assortment of self-serving words. Using a script of any kind in any negotiation proves that you have not been listening.

- If a negotiation is not working out in your favor, don't compromise and give away what you cannot afford to give away. That includes your value and self-respect. Be willing to walk away.

- Don't focus on the outcome of any negotiation at first. Focus on the process instead.

- Just ask. But ask once you've laid a foundation for doing so and have earned the right to.

- Listen with your *soul*. Listening with your soul involves listening with your ears, your eyes, your body and your hearts. Don't engage in the act of partial listening. Leave your ego behind.

- Never judge or accuse, especially in negotiations.

- When listening soulfully, use encouragers such as "uh - huh," "go on" and nodding your head to encourage the other to continue talking. Paraphrase when you are not clear about what was just being said.

- Life is too complicated and dynamic to follow a script. Whenever possible, never use a cast-in-stone script. Rehearsing is fine which I will discuss in greater detail (role-play) but *reading* from a script is a no-no.

Call to Action:

As with my keynote talks, not only do I summarize my main points for my audiences as I have just done for you, but I leave them with a call to action: something they can immediately do to apply the principles they've just been introduced to. That's what I will do for you as well with your 'calls to action.'

- From this point on, be aware of what your body language is conveying to your negotiatee. When meeting someone, are you standing straight with your shoulders back with a posture that conveys confidence? Are you smiling, using eye contact and showing genuine interest? Be aware of what your body is 'saying' to the one you're with, and make whatever changes need to be made to convey confidence. Watch theirs as well. What is their body telling you?

- Never be in a rush to finish the negotiation. Next time you find yourself in a negotiation, no matter if it's in life or in business, don't rush it. Be respectful of their time, of course, and work within whatever time you are blessed to have, but don't rush. If you can't reach every point because of time restraints, say so. Ask to pick it up at another time and express your reasons for asking to do so.

- Next time you want to influence a decision or have something work out in both your mutual interests, talk less. Put the focus on the one you're with. Ask them to tell you how they see things from their point of view.

- Have you been putting off asking for something? A raise, a date, a job? Stop waiting. It's time for you to 'just ask.' Lay the foundation. Plan now to see that someone and give them reasons to say 'yes.'

And now that we have examined some guideposts and principles involved in successful negotiating and asking, it's time to introduce you to the PIER™. Many of these principles will be explained even further as we go along.

PART 4

BUILD A BRIDGE AND THEY WILL BE HAPPY TO CROSS IT.

Chapter Three

———•◆•———

PIER™ PRINCIPLE NUMBER 1: PLANNING

The 'P' in PIER™ Negotiating – Planning

My daughter, Aimée, planned her wedding for several months in advance, and because of that well thought out planning, the ceremony and celebration of her commitment to the love of her life, Matthew, unfolded flawlessly. The witnesses who attended their celebration of love are still talking about how wonderfully it turned out.

Planning a wedding involves planning several months in advance, often more than a year, and includes a multitude of important steps. These steps include planning details such as: starting a wedding binder or folder, working out a budget, picking a wedding party, picking the date and location, creating a guest list, reserving dates and venues, booking an officiant, hiring a photographer and/or videographer, booking the entertainment, meeting caterers, choosing and purchasing a dress, creating a website, picking invitations, sending invitations, picking flowers, sampling food, rehearsals and much more.

Using the above example, for instance, serves to highlight the importance of being completely prepared for important events (and negotiations) that matter to you, be it in life or business. There are so many important details to consider, and neglecting any one of these vital steps, as in the wedding example I just provided, can make the difference between a happily-ever-after day to remember and a not-so-happy one. A great deal rides on this special day, and I salute every woman who prepares for it. It's a lot of work, but it also means so much.

I was never a bride, nor am I ever going to be a bride-to-be. But I certainly can appreciate the vast amount of work that my daughter, and every other woman, including many of you reading, have put into the planning phase of this memorable day. By planning thoroughly, accounting for every minute detail, you stand a greater chance of achieving your desired outcomes more frequently.

The same is true in other life matters and in business. Using the wedding example above, what similarities can we draw that apply to your life and business negotiations?

1. **Starting a wedding binder or folder:** For you, it may be creating a client file, or in life matters, a diary or written plan.

2. **Working out a budget:** This not only applies to business but to life as well. In business, it translates to knowing what your bottom dollar is; how much you can afford to accept as your bottom line for the cost of your product and services. In life, it may simply be what you're prepared to negotiate as your salary, not accepting a dollar less. It comes down to your value.

3. **Picking a wedding party:** In business, this involves picking your best negotiator and your team. In life, it may be picking someone to run your ideas by or role-play with.

4. **Picking a date and location:** Whether in life or business, consider where the meeting takes place and when. Choosing a

spot with the least amount of interruptions is extremely important.

5. **Choosing a dress:** No matter who or under what circumstances, knowing how to dress for the meeting and dressing accordingly will help make a establish that good first impression. Not all meetings call for the same outfit.

6. **Rehearsal:** As you're about to discover, rehearsal is one of the physical preparation steps that helps ensure your important meeting goes off without a hitch. It involves role-play, such as the exercise I spoke of earlier with Jacques.

These are but a few similarities we can draw from the wedding example that will help you be your best prepared you. Now, let's examine preparation more closely.

Up to this point, you've been introduced to several negotiation and asking concepts as well as these three guideposts: No manipulating; Just ask and Listen with your soul. The 'You listen to me,' intimidating or manipulative approaches to negotiating, be it in life or business, are not only self-sabotaging but they will have long-standing negative consequences. Fear of rejection or of being told 'no' are jailors who have no right to keep you locked in cages. They will prevent you from moving forward and from reaching what you want and deserve in life. You and you alone hold the key to your self-made prisons, and you have an inherent right to go for what we want in life.

You've now reached the PIER™. The next four chapters will be devoted to the principles behind each letter of PIER™. These are your anchors to successful negotiating and asking. Follow these principles and consider PIER™ the path that leads you to the lighthouse.

Let's begin with the first principle: The P in PIER™.

Planning and preparedness are the first steps along the PIER™

Whenever possible, the first thing we should do before we enter any negotiation, be it in life or in business, is to **plan and prepare** for it. We've all heard this warning: fail to plan, plan to fail. It makes sense to prepare

> "By failing to plan, you are planning to fail."
>
> ~ Benjamin Franklin

for just about everything else in life, like planning a trip, preparing for a test, planning a holiday feast and so on, so planning your ask or negotiation also makes sense.

Experience has proven that there are tremendous rewards for preparing well. Some studies suggest that as much as 80% of the key to success in any project is planning. I'm a bit more conservative than that. In my experience, I'd say that at least 50% to 60% of the key to my success in any of my hostage negotiations and criminal interrogations has been planning.

By planning, I mean *preparedness* - planning mentally, physically and practically for the negotiation. For best results, you really owe it to both yourself and your negotiatee to be as prepared as possible. A well-planned approach to any goal will increase your chances of achieving success.

Strategic planning

No successful professional undertakes any task without having a plan and a specific goal in mind. Being without a solid vision, plan or goal is like trying to find your way through an unfamiliar bustling city without a guide of any kind. It's easy to get lost. Your purpose in whatever negotiation you enter must be specific, yet simple. You must have a clear plan before you enter any negotiation. It must include your promise of service to others: your clients, your customers and your negotiatees.

> No successful professional undertakes any task without having a plan and specific goal in mind. Being without a solid vision, plan or goal is like trying to find your way through a busy city you're unfamiliar with without a map. It's easy to get lost.

Planning mentally, physically and practically for the negotiation

Before we begin to negotiate and engage with others in the art of asking, it's imperative that we work on ourselves first. Planning involves being prepared mentally, physically and practically for the negotiation, encounter or meeting. It requires that we look deep into ourselves, critically, and that we become our best-prepared selves first, so that we may confidently move forward to negotiate and influence successfully with others.

Self-evaluation

I urge you, in preparation for that meeting and/or negotiation, in addition to finding out as much as possible about your negotiatee, evaluate yourself first. Self-examination and self-discovery are important considerations in helping you prepare for your meeting, no matter what it may be and with whom. These are also important steps to help you determine whether you've become a victim of self-sabotage (or are currently in a state of) and need to escape any self-sabotaging thought captors that may be holding you back from advancing confidently and effortlessly with the negotiation or meeting with your negotiatee.

***

Take a hard look in the mirror at the person staring back at you. Do you like what you see? Would you do business or agree to what they ask you for? If not, do some fine tuning.

***

We often put too much freakin' stress on ourselves. Self-evaluation involves taking an honest and hard look at not only our strengths, but our weaknesses just as importantly, including our self-sabotaging beliefs, and should we uncover those beasts, on working on ridding ourselves of them. We need strengths and not weaknesses to succeed, and so we must cut out that which does not serve us, be it a habit, a thought or a combination of both.

Self-evaluation involves working on ourselves and believing that we are just as worthy as anyone else out there to get what we're after **and** that we are just as important as our negotiatee. If we believe we have something of value for our negotiatee, then we must consciously realize that if they've agreed to provide us their time, then they must be interested in meeting us and in hearing what we have to offer them. Remember – you could be the answer to their dreams.

Believing that they are interested in us and what we have to offer as much as we are interested in them is extremely important in preparation, for it helps build that much-needed confidence. This could be anything from a business meeting to a first date.

If someone agrees to give us their time than they're interested in finding out more about something we have. Think about it: someone has said 'yes' to meeting you. It could be a manager, a business owner or someone you've asked out on a date. Imagine what happens to *them* once they've make the agreement to meet you. They've scheduled you into their day. They may have altered some of their original plans. In the example of meeting for a date, they're choosing what to wear, how to greet you, what to say and on and on. No different than you, is it now? Same applies in business and in other life negotiations.

You have unlimited power. It's only limited if you choose it to be

You know how I said you're damn near limitless? You are. Just think about it. You have the ability to turn your fears into courage. You have the power to choose positive self-talk over negative self-talk. To succeed in asking and negotiating, begin by telling yourself that you have *every right* to ask for what you want once you've built the foundation for doing so, and believe it. Be confident in yourself. Self-confidence attracts people – it's part of that charisma I spoke of earlier. It's a golden thread in the law of attraction.

We've all suffered self-doubt or loss of confidence at some point in our lives, but there are ways to move beyond it. You're not unique in your fears, self-doubt or in having butterflies before you meet and greet that certain someone, deliver a proposal or whatever.

I still get nervous the moment before I go on stage to deliver a keynote talk for example, and others I've spoken to who are entertainers or do the same as I do say those butterflies never leave them either. But what does happen for those such as I who know how to move beyond that nervousness and fear is that they/we accept it as a reminder of the importance of what we're about to do.

And the moment we connect with that feeling and choose to move beyond it - despite it, we become magically and instantly energized. In a fraction of a second it disappears and is replaced with focus and professional delivery.

I remember when I'd been chosen to deliver my TEDx talk in Toronto, Canada in October of 2015. Man was I excited! What an honor. The TEDx people I worked with were professional and wonderful to work with, and they want the very best talks to be delivered to the millions who expect and look forward to the same. To accomplish this, they pair writing coaches with their speakers and months of preparation go into each individual talk so that on the day of event, in front of a live audience of one thousand people, with several cameras capturing it, broadcasting to thousands more, the speaker will knock it out of the ball park! Right? That's the idea.

Now I'll admit that this is one of those rare instances where script memorization applies. It's entertainment after all. TED talks are delivered in six, twelve and eighteen-minute segments, depending on the topic, so you just can't 'wing it' if you expect to get all your keynote points out to the listeners within the allotment of time you've been provided. Mine was chosen as an eighteen-minute talk, which meant I had to stick as close to that eighteen-minute slot as possible.

My writing coach helped me plan content, and once I'd written my talk, timed it and modified it to fit my; allotment of time, I memorized it as I would a movie script so that it would sound as natural and unrehearsed as possible. The last thing I wanted was to turn off my audience and have it sound memorized. It would not have sounded authentic and natural, and that would not have made the impact I'd set out to make. Nor would it have left audiences feeling satisfied with what they'd heard. I worked on it day and night for three months – yes, hours and hours.

The day came to deliver our talks and mine was chosen as the last one of the day. Now that's a sweet spot for any speaker because it's the message the attendees will be left with at the very end of the day. It's a prime spot; but for a speaker, me in this case, it meant I had to wait all day to deliver my talk. Talk about stress. To say I felt I had butterflies would be an understatement. I had a kaleidoscope of them! The day seemed to take forever, although I was enjoying each moment of it with family and friends, listening to the talks my colleagues before me were delivering.

Midway through the afternoon, I was led to a waiting room away from the auditorium where the speakers who had delivered their talks were gathered to relax, unwind and celebrate their accomplishments. There were television monitors delivering live feeds of the event so we could watch the other speakers delivering their talks. My time was approaching, one stressful minute at a time.

I wasn't a professional keynote speaker back then. That came after my TED talk. I'd never spoken to such a large audience before and what I was about to say would now become a permanent record for millions to access on various internet sites, should they so choose, until the end of days. What if I stumbled? What if I forgot everything I was going to say? What if I messed up? What if no one liked it? Well, as I said earlier, we can 'what-if' ourselves forever and listen to those 'what-if's' as they imprison us in not doing what we set out to do and should do. I now know better, but it happens to even the most experienced of us, but it's quashed almost as immediately as it arrives by true professionals who may still experience it on occasion.

It happened to me that afternoon. As the minutes ticked away, I was getting closer to show time. I was led to the 'green-room,' a room right next to the stage so that I would only have a few steps to take before reaching center stage when it was my time to speak. The speaker on stage was three minutes from finishing up. I was next. I could see her from where I sat through a curtain.

As I sat there, it happened. My heart was pounding so hard in my chest that I couldn't hear myself think. And I then realized, much to my horror…I'd forgotten all my lines. Every last one of them! I had no idea what I was going to say. Months of rehearsal unexpectedly and devastatingly vanished. I was clueless. Not even my opening line was coming back to me. I felt doomed. I was experiencing the 'fight-or-flight' syndrome real bad, and an overwhelming sense of fear had now taken me hostage.

Over the beating sound of my heart, I could faintly hear the sound of applause coming from the auditorium as the last speaker made her exit and walked into the green room where I sat waiting for execution. The master of ceremonies was now introducing his next speaker – me, for goodness sakes. A nod came my way from the MC, indicating it was show time. I stood up, took a deep breath and decided that very second that I was not a hostage to fear. I reminded myself that I'd prepared extensively for this moment and that my sudden memory loss was only temporary, and I attributed it to simple nervousness. It was time to kill that monster.

I moved confidently forward, despite my earlier fear, and do you know what? The moment I stepped onto that stage and saw the audience, each person there to hear the magic of the spoken word, many who *wanted* to hear my message, I immediately became energized. The moment I stepped onto the stage, my nervousness disappeared. I had killed that monster and moved forward, despite my nervousness. I reminded myself, "You've got this!" The butterflies had flown off to watch the show. My first line was there, waiting for me, as was the second, the third, the fourth and every line from there on in. I had an amazing time delivering my talk and received a standing ovation for it. What a memorable and wonderful day!

In examining this as it applies to your world, what lessons can we draw from my TEDx experience? Much like planning a wedding, as I went over earlier. Right?!

- **Involving a team:** For one, working with someone else (or a team) as you prepare for your life or business negotiation will not only help you prepare, it will help you 'feel' prepared. In this case, I had a writing and vocal coach assigned to me. Both helped me prepare to be my best so that on the big day, I'd deliver my best to my 'clients' (the audience, in this case). Whether in life or in business, consider involving others in helping you 'feel' prepared. Especially when the stakes of the negotiation are high.

- **Preparation often involves time:** I studied for hours and hours, well in advance. What is it you can 'study' for? It may be as simple as researching who you'll be meeting with, what values or expectations they have, knowing your product and services inside and out, being prepared to vocalize your strengths and what you have to offer, going over your proposal and so forth.

- **Rehearsal:** I rehearsed in front of a small audience more than once. These were my fellow speakers, the TEDx team and guests they had invited a day before the scheduled event.

- **Moving forward despite fear and nervousness:** It happens to all of us. As you saw from my example, I thought I'd forgotten everything seconds before I stepped on stage. But I hadn't. I was so well prepared that the moment I reminded myself of this, the stress disappeared. The moment

I stepped on stage, it all came back to me in an energized, beautiful way.

Now let's examine your world more in depth for a moment. One important tool to access in those moments of doubt and nervousness is asking *yourself* the right kind of questions to help you understand your motivations, values, and direction. As you'll discover in Chapter 4 (The I in PIER™ – Intent) having the right motivation and intent is imperative. For instance, asking yourself, "What do I want from this meeting?" or "What do I have of real value to offer my negotiatee?" is a good habit to get into while preparing. It helps you focus and stay on task.

By examining yourself fully and honestly, and by asking yourself the right pre-negotiation questions, you can then choose to apply positive thought-change, adjust purposeful actions, re-direct thoughts and get to where you want and need to be – out of whatever hostaged mindset you may find yourself in to move confidently into the negotiation or meeting. In the story I just shared with you about my TED talk, I'm the one who momentarily sabotaged myself almost to the point of paralyzation.

It happens to all of us from time to time. But in my case, it was only momentary because I deployed my positive self-talk to remind myself that I had well prepared for that talk and had to move beyond my temporary fear. I had to remind myself: "You've got this!"

Sure, I and a number of other people can tell you what to do. But simply listening to a positive message given by a motivational speaker or coach is simply not enough. The responsibility lies with you to make it all happen. I can only provide you guidance, and as I mentioned much earlier at the very beginning of this book, the only one who can rescue you from your self-sabotaging ways or from that rock of solitude and hopelessness you find yourself on, is you. I did, and I have.

You must believe what positive thing you tell yourself and then act on it. This involves examining yourself to see if there is something that's been holding you back from being the very best you can be in your chosen profession – or in life, before asking for what you want. Only you hold the key to the cages that keep you hostage – use it.

> When we expose our weaknesses but aren't prepared to work on them, that inaction leads to stress. The pitfall to that is that nothing changes, and life goes on its unfulfilled way.

An unexamined life is an unexamined life – much may need to be improved but won't

Ancient Greek philosopher, Socrates, once said, "The life that is unexamined is not worth living."[16]

Unfortunately, most people avoid leading an examined life. It's not that they don't have time to examine themselves, their circumstances or current states. But many actively avoid doing so. The fear of exposing flaws, shortcomings and bad attitudes is downright terrifying to many. When we expose our weaknesses but aren't prepared to work on them, that inaction leads to stress.

The pitfall to that is that nothing changes, and life goes on its unfulfilled way. In your case, you may remain immobilized in your negotiations and in your life. You don't get what you want if you

---

[16] Plato's Apology

don't ask for what you want; and at the end of that unfulfilled life, the individual will look back on his or her unfulfilled life and ask, "What was I thinking?" By then it will be too late. The ghosts of missed opportunities who visit won't be kind then.

People who examine their lives to reflect upon where they've been, where they are and where they're going are by far much happier people. None of us has all the answers. No one's life is free from trouble and strife. But those who have a sense of where they belong in the universe and know their value at least have some understanding of how all the elements fit together and know what they should and can do to create their own destinies and put their troubles and conflicts behind them. Their success lies, in part, to self-evaluation.

Self-examination is not unlike a blueprint which capitalizes on our strengths and helps us discover our weaknesses. It also helps us appreciate what we *do* have. Once we study that blueprint, we'll have a much greater chance of creating and designing a map for ourselves to get us get to where we want to be and to get what we want and deserve.

When we take time to examine our lives, professional *and personal,* and in this case our lives as negotiators and askers, it also stands to reason that we'll make time to work on improving it. We must create and use our own new and improved maps to get us to where we want to be. The two go hand in hand, in lock-step.

One of the most difficult things about examining our lives is getting started. I encourage you to get started before your next meeting. One of the greatest discoveries I made in police work as you now know was when I realized that the person standing or sitting across from me was just like me. They're likely wondering the same thing I am: "Is this the best thing for me?"

Remember, we share more similarities than we do differences; and when I placed myself in my clients' shoes, I came to understand them better, providing me with a better opportunity to serve them and get what I was after in return. Before you meet with your negotiatee, be it your client or whoever, ask yourself if you've done everything you possibly could have to prepare for it. Examine yourself before you examine them.

Behaving naturally and humanly helps build bridges

What I'm about to suggest may sound a bit odd, but stay with me on this. It involves human nature and how we interact with one other. I don't want to be misunderstood by suggesting that you look unprofessional at any given moment in the negotiation room or when meeting someone new. On the contrary. I want you to remain professional always, or in the case of meeting someone new, composed, always. But don't be afraid to show your humanness. In fact, find ways to do precisely that.

In business, consider borrowing a pen. Borrow a piece of paper. Do something human and make light of it. In life, and when meeting someone new, don't *try* to be perfect. You might drop something, spill a little something and laugh about it. Don't go overboard. Just be you – imperfect and beautiful. And don't worry - just about everybody wants to deal with or be with someone who is just like them, another human being just like themselves… someone with whom they can feel connected, and someone they can relate to and even help. They've been there too. They've forgotten a pen, a piece of paper or spilled a little something. By helping you, they'll feel better about themselves and see you more as themselves - an equal at the table.

***
Dare to be your beautiful self, no matter what
***

Being yourself establishes connection. It also helps to break down barriers that may exist between negotiating people. The next time you're involved in a negotiation of any kind, be your beautiful badass self. Some of the greatest negotiators in the world use this "I'm not perfect" method to help break down barriers. And once you do use it, tell me you don't see an immediate change in the atmosphere and relationship your building with the other individual. You will.

I've read that one of the strategies many psychiatrists have used in the past to make their new patients feel more comfortable and at ease was to sit across from them in their office as they gathered their papers and "accidentally" spill their coffee over their papers. Then they would clumsily reach for paper towels to clean up the mess while smiling and joking about how clumsy they'd just been. You may wonder if this approach works. Remarkably, the research indicates that it does[17]. The patient sitting across from the doctor suddenly saw the doctor as someone very much like themselves - a human being they could connect to, identify with and trust. It demonstrated vulnerability and showed the patient that their doctor was indeed a fallible human being, much like themselves, which remarkably helps build trust. This approach just works.

---

[17] https://ind.pn/2KCBhSD

Dealing with self-sabotage: an absolute must before you move forward along the PIER™

While still in preparation we must deal with self-sabotage. I've mentioned this a few times and believe it to be important enough to explore it more in depth now, since self-sabotage, which is directly linked to self-doubt, will critically mess up your chances of success in all your life and business negotiations. What I know about people from my line of work is this: we all experience self-sabotage at some point. So, let's deal with any self-sabotage and/or self-doubt in the **planning** phase.

One of the challenges some face that can affect winning or losing in the field of negotiations and life is how well they deal with that self-doubt, and what actions they take because of it. You can't let a past failure, or a fear of failure, comparison or judgement stop you from moving ahead in negotiations and in life. That's self-sabotage. It's a roadblock you just don't need.

I believe in being fearless; but I understand that for many, fear often never disappears unless the one experiencing fear learns to overcome it: or at the very least, manages to control it. The secret to success over fear is to move beyond it, despite your fears. Fake it until you make it if you must. I did that afternoon of my TED talk, and the results were well worth the exercise of doing so. I attribute being able to do so by the amount of preparation I'd put into it as well.

Deal with whatever roadblocks and self-sabotaging behaviors you may have and act with confidence moving forward. Take risks, embrace opportunities and by all means move forward. Even though you may not have the confidence it takes to meet that new person or to enter that negotiation, fake it if you must. Become an actor and rehearse extensively for it. You'll discover how to do this more in the section on role-playing. The more you do something, the easier it becomes. It will become second nature.

Again, dealing with your self-sabotaging behaviors is an absolute must. Your past does not have to equal your future. You are not bound by past mistakes or experiences. They're in the past, and you are not your past. You can create new empowering beliefs for yourself. Begin to believe in possibilities as opposed to failures. Believe in your value and believe that you are limitless. Then behave as such.

Know your worth

Knowing your value and knowing when to move forward and when to walk away makes you a winner. Undercutting yourself devalues you, and you end up losing, no matter what you're after. Remember the Lisbon, Portugal story I told you about? It takes self-confidence and an understanding of human nature to know when to push ahead and when to back away, no matter what the circumstances. Without developing the confidence-to-negotiate or to ask for what you want in life, you'll fail to accomplish the results you seek.

The more you practice and apply the principles of PIER™ negotiating, the more confidence you'll have and the more successful you'll become. It's that simple.

Emotions, instincts and insights help you connect with the person you're negotiating with, and fear has no place at the negotiation table or when asking or meeting anyone. Only confidence does – that, and the right solution for your negotiatee.

Consider, again, that what you ask or propose to your negotiatee may be exactly what your negotiatee wants. However, without asking, you'll never know. Not asking ensures the answer to be 'no'.

Being aware that you have a right to ask for what you want once you've established the groundwork and followed the steps to do so is a must. You wouldn't walk up to a complete stranger and without so much as an introduction ask that person out or ask the person for a coffee, a drink, or whatever **and** expect to get a 'yes,' would you? That's the jack-in-the-box approach.

In that kind of situation, a nice chat first would go a long way toward reaching a yes. Springing the question without laying the foundation is not going to get you far. For a better chance at a 'yes,' you must always lay the groundwork first (the foundation on which to move forward). Build a bridge or tear down a wall and then build a bridge. That's the professional and personal relationship approach.

Ok, ok, "What wall are you talking about Paul? Where did that come from? I just met the person, how could there be a wall already?" is what you may be thinking. We all have walls. We prefer to keep people at a safe and comfortable distance until we choose to let them in closer. I believe the average 'personal space' wall is three feet? You know what yours is, I'm certain of that. We all have one.

Instinctively, we are conditioned to be cautious when meeting someone for the first time. Our primitive brains have taught us to evaluate strangers and ask ourselves, "Friend, foe or someone I can procreate with? Can I eat it, can it eat me, or is this a potential partner?[18]" is how we were conditioned to think.

Not too much has changed since then other than we don't look at the person we're just meeting and wonder whether they're going to eat us, but we do wonder whether they are a threat to us.

---

[18] Mark Bowden, friend, body language expert and founder of "Truth Plane" www.truthplane.com

In business, when you meet someone new, it's only natural to wonder whether they have your best interests in mind. Many business people naturally wonder whether the person they're dealing may try to take advantage

> **You are not bound by past mistakes or experiences. They are in the past, and you are not your past.**

of them. And if you're dating someone for the first time, of course you'll be examining them to determine whether they're safe for you. It's not only human nature to do so; it's wise. Doing so will provide you a greater chance of remaining safe and alive.

Our primitive brain was designed to help protect us and signals us to any hint of danger, risk and often insincerity. This applies as much to meeting someone for a first-time encounter as it does to meeting someone for a first-time business opportunity. Timing is very important when it comes to asking. You must establish the foundation and relationship first, however brief that may be, and it doesn't have to be a long drawn out affair. Relationships can develop quickly, depending on how good you are at building them.

Grab negotiation opportunities by the throat and don't let go

Many of us miss an abundance of great opportunities to improve our lives through negotiation (or asking) simply because we don't look for - or see - these opportunities to do so, even when they're staring us right in the face. Remember my Oprah story? Why this is so may come down to not knowing what to look for, or it may simply be that we haven't considered even trying. Some of us deliberately avoid opportunity because of whatever fear we may associate to it. 'Opportunities' are circumstances that present themselves providing us a chance to do something that will undoubtedly benefit us.

Admittedly, we don't always see opportunities coming – it's not like they wear neon signs announcing themselves pre-arrival. We often *miss* them because we don't recognize them. We may *avoid* them because we fear them – or more specifically, we fear the action it will take to turn that opportunity into success. ("What if's" again.) In the language of negotiations, it's not only ideal to plan, it's vital.

As you know, planning is the first principle in the PIER™ Negotiation model. Yes, most negotiations we plan for ahead of time. Those are the ones we know are coming or those we create for ourselves. They are specific: by that I mean you will already know who you'll be negotiating with, what for, and what your intended outcome is. But other negotiation 'opportunities' sometimes blindside us – we just won't have all the facts and they smack us upside the head. They are the ones we stumble upon or suddenly find ourselves in unexpectedly. It's our job then to slow it down and get the facts.

Negotiating is as much a part of each of our daily lives as is breathing. Opportunities to negotiate arise daily. Once you study the principles of negotiation found here and practice them consistently, you'll develop a heightened sense of awareness and you'll be more equipped to see opportunity when it presents itself. Knowing how to deal with whatever comes your way gives you the edge to succeed and the vision to see. Opportunities appear in different forms to everyone.

***

Begin looking for opportunities to ask and negotiate for what you want. If there aren't any, create them.

***

Role-playing: a *physical* planning

In hostage and crisis negotiations, we rarely knew what call or crisis was coming next. So, we would regularly prepare for the unexpected by running realistic mock scenarios to practice and keep sharp. Our training was ongoing. These realistic and evaluated *role-play* scenarios involved professional actors and all levels of emergency services. I suggest, and you may either like or hate the idea, that you start role-playing before your next ask or negotiation. It really is a blast and get's you charged on top of that.

Here's how it worked for us: once or twice a month, we'd attend a full-days' training session at which time we were handed a random scenario to deal with. We were evaluated on how effectively we handled the negotiation. Often the scenarios would run for hours, depending on the expertise of the negotiator and the situation. This meant that we had to be prepared to negotiate under *any* given circumstance and condition - whether it was a hostage-taker holding a busload of children at gunpoint demanding a ransom, or a suicidal individual threatening to jump off a bridge.

Business Bulletin # 6:

You, the business negotiator, have an advantage in that you know before going into a meeting what type of negotiation you'll be involved in. This allows you the opportunity to role-play and prepare beforehand. For those of you who are planning a life negotiation, this applies to you just as well. Think about asking a friend or your partner to play the role of the negotiatee you'll be meeting ahead of time as a 'practice run.'

That might involve role-playing for a job interview or whatever else is of importance to you. Role-playing allows you to work in realistic mock situations in which you play the role of the negotiator and/or asker, and your partner plays the role of the negotiatee and vise-versa. This strategy worked extremely well for my colleagues and I. Reverse the roles occasionally and have fun with it. Do it often and critique yourselves honestly. Do it until you get it right. Perfect practice makes perfect.

This strategy requires homework. What might your negotiatee ask you, and what's your answer going to be? Think of all they might ask you and/or whatever objections they may have; and have your answers prepared and committed solidly to memory in advance, so much so that it will not sound like a static script I warned you about. That way they'll come out flawlessly without sounding rehearsed.

To master anything, a great deal of practice is necessary. They say that "practice makes perfect." More accurately, *perfect* practice makes perfect. If you practice something you're doing wrong repeatedly, no matter how much you practice, you'll still get it wrong. Practice first how to do it right and then practice doing it repeatedly until it becomes second nature.

Your goal will be to do it so often you don't need to think much about it. It will come easily to you. Like that dream sports car and a precise map to whichever destination you choose I told you at the onset of this book. Having both will help you navigate through what first appears to be a complex series of highways and roadblocks but the more you travel that road, (in this case, the more you role-play), the more familiar it becomes and the more easily it becomes to get to where you want to be. Delivery is so much easier when you're prepared and well-rehearsed.

Business Bulletin # 7: know your client *and* your competition ahead of time

In business especially, find out as much as you can about who you will be negotiating with – *and* who your competition is. For me as a hostage negotiator, I wanted to know everything I possibly could about the person I was negotiating with or the suspect I was about to interrogate.

In hostage negotiations, I didn't have the benefit of investigating the hostage-taker before I received a call, but I did have a team of experienced investigators that were deployed to go out and obtain the crucial information I needed to gain an insight into who I was dealing with. While I was busy negotiating, vital intelligence was being handed to me.

Ten minutes on Google or LinkedIn can provide you a rich amount of immediate, ready-to-use intelligence that will stand you in good stead as you prepare to meet your client or prospect.

Because of the urgency and unexpected nature of each call (it's not like we made an appointment a week in advance with hostage-takers or suicidal persons) I relied on that team of qualified detectives to help to me with that crucial task. You too must make use of your team if you have one available.

You may or may not have a team or have administrative support to help you. If you do, you can have someone do the "back story" investigation on your client or target, or you can work at doing it together. If not, ten minutes on Google or LinkedIn can get you a rich amount of immediate, ready-to-use intelligence that will stand you in good stead as you prepare to meet your client or prospect. Take a page from the Investment Advisers Copybook: "Know your Client." You might get a better idea of what he/she is looking for, and you'll have a better idea whether you and your company can provide the service or product they want and need – or even something different and better.

Before you waste your time and theirs, you must absolutely believe in your product or service and honestly assess whether it's a fit for your client. Obviously, you must buy into your own services and products first if you're to convince anyone else that they should buy into them. If you don't believe in what you're selling or offering, you're not likely to succeed. If that's the case, find a way to believe in at least some feature, function or benefit of the product or service you offer. That's all part of business-negotiation preparation.

In life negotiations, what is *your* product? It's you, of course. You must absolutely believe in yourself and what you have to offer before meeting with whoever you'll negotiate/interact with. Know what value you can bring to them. Make yourself your best product – one you believe in.

***

Believe in yourself first and others will
believe in you too.

***

One of the things you should do to create an advantage for yourself is to discover as much as you can about your negotiatee before you first meet. This applies to your life negotiations just as well. Knowing as much about the person and/or organization you'll be dealing with before you embark on any negotiation will be of immense value to you and will help the overall negotiation go smoother. Why? Because for one, you'll discover valuable intelligence about them and what they're about before you even start talking.

You may discover what values their company embraces by reading their mission statement, for example, providing you with insight into their goals and objectives, creating one of many 'advantage points' you need to succeed. By doing so, you might want to tell them that you've read and appreciated their mission statement when you first meet to begin to establish that much-needed rapport, thereby easing into "conversation mode" before you get right down to the discussion of what's being negotiated. The importance of doing so cannot be overvalued.

Building rapport involves giving your negotiatee your attention, being positive, and coordinating your thoughts and concerns with those of your negotiatee. It is no surprise that rapport relies heavily on active listening as I repeatedly observe throughout this work for good reason. For rapport building to be effective, you have to ensure your verbal and nonverbal communication is in harmony. The latter includes your voice tone, using open-handed gestures, and having eye contact. Listen with your eyes, ears, body, and soul.

Emotion in the negotiation

As negotiators and askers trying to influence behavioral change in our negotiatees, it's necessary to first understand the current state of emotions in which your negotiatees find themselves in and assess their behavior from there. Empathy helps accomplish just that - seeing and understanding the perspective of another by seeing things from their point of view. To be an effective negotiator you must invite your negotiatee to speak and demonstrate empathy by taking time to listen (yes, a pattern is developing here - each of these skills work in tandem with each other quite nicely). As earlier noted, what hostage negotiators have come to discover is that *emotion* plays a significant role in *every* successful negotiation; and empathy is a sure way to explore emotion.

Omitting emotion or failing to empathize will be counterproductive to any of your negotiations. Emotion, an essential element when identified and handled correctly, is a core element in all successful negotiations. Showing empathy helps build relationships and encourages connection and cooperation. Exercising empathy along with a genuine desire to understand what the other individual is experiencing is a must in every negotiation. When a person *feels* appreciated and understood, they are more likely to express their needs and concerns. And that's exactly what you want to discover so that you will be provided with a complete understanding of what is needed and how you can deliver it.

What's the difference between negotiating with a hostage-taker demanding a large sum of cash and a hard-ass businessman trying to intimidate his negotiatee into accepting something that is clearly unacceptable? Other than the fact that in the hostage situation you can't walk away, the answer is: not *that* much. In some instances, the professional hostage-taker, after all, is simply a businessman trying to get the best deal - depending obviously on circumstances.

Whether a bank robber making demands after taking a hostage or a business shark trying to take advantage of the negotiatee sitting across from him/her, there's very little "listening that takes place" - originally. Like a conversation, there must never be a hardened script. Instead, it should involve building the relationship, one in which two or more people work together to fully listen to and understand each other and their needs before a deal is struck. Using this method, the person you're negotiating with is more open to working towards a "Yes."

This book as you've likely discovered by now is all about those very techniques and steps to help influence and establish the right kind of relationship and rapport needed to succeed. It's a calculated, friendly approach to influencing behavioral change. Gone are the days of approaching life and business negotiations with a mindset of always "getting down to business" and going solely for what *we* want, if you plan to succeed.

If we approach negotiation with only our needs and wants first and foremost, without involving our negotiatee in the process and demonstrating some value to them in hearing us out, we invite a solid and unshakable "No" from whomever we're negotiating with. And that's a 'No' that you may never recover from. I've seen that approach used in the line of duty more than once as unskilled interrogators aggressively went after confessions from a suspect, by-passing any rapport-building and going for the juggler with the same old line, "We know you did it, so just tell us what we want to know!" Yeah, right. Like the suspect is going to give it all up on an approach like that. Not freakin' likely.

History has taught us that early hostage negotiation techniques focusing on self-serving, aggressive tactics that demanded the hostage-taker surrender (as snipers set their guns to take them out) like the tactics my fellow cops used in their interrogation approaches just didn't work.

The skilled and successful interrogator, hostage negotiator and business negotiator have come a heck of a long way in understanding that people need and deserve to be treated as living, emotional individuals. And the negotiatee sitting across from you deserves the same. Only then does cooperation have a way to surface and exist. Demonstrating empathy, understanding, and a willingness to see things from another's point of view is vital - no matter what kind of negotiation you undertake.

We are, after all, emotional and often irrational creatures who base many of our decisions, behaviors, choices and actions on how we "feel" as opposed to solely basing them on facts. If we feel intimidated, unheard and unappreciated, we close up and disengage. In the case of a business deal or even a sale, the potential client says they have to 'think about it' or the customer says she's 'just looking.'

Business bulletin # 8:

In business, we look for solutions and agreements - but before we reach agreements and commitments regardless of what's at stake, we instinctively look for an emotional link that satisfies us that we're dealing with the right person and making the best choice we can, given the circumstances at hand. It's no different in life negotiations. We all have an inherent need to be heard, acknowledged and understood.

Should the opposite occur, it contradicts the establishment of trust in the relationship, and our thoughts lead to the belief that either the other person's trying to "put one over on us," or they just haven't bothered to listen and consider our concerns and feelings in the slightest. When that happens, those little voices in our heads start shouting, telling us that the negotiatee across from us just isn't listening - and those voices tune out the other individual because our needs and concerns haven't been validated. When that happens, that negotiation or business transaction is over. We fold our cards, step away from the negotiating table and find the nearest exit. It's human nature.

Label that emotion before it bites you in the ass

Occasionally, 'white elephant' will drop by the negotiation to make an appearance. I mentioned those beasts a bit earlier. 'White elephants' are what I consider 'sudden and unexpected moments of discomfort or unexpected emotion' that may arise during the negotiation.

Once considered a gift you gave to annoy the hell out of someone – something the recipient could not easily get rid of, 'white elephants' now wander the negotiation world looking for places to visit. They're negotiation snatchers: appearing as a moment when the atmosphere, body language and/or words and tone used suddenly change from one moment to the next because of what is now being – or not being – said or discussed. A nerve has been struck and it needs to be dealt with now, and not later. White elephants enter the minds of your negotiatee and wait to see what you'll do.

Don't fear them – they shouldn't be considered unwelcomed. They're very much welcome, should they pop in, so make them at home – for as short a visit as possible. They'll go away on their own accord providing you address them with the respect they deserve and attention they're after. Once you identify an unexpected emotion shift for example (one of the white elephants), you won't ignore it. Slow things down immediately by identifying and addressing the emotion you've sensed just dropped in. Only then will the white elephant be satisfied. How you handle the white elephant will dictate how long they'll stay.

For example, if your negotiatee becomes suddenly upset by something you just said, identify the emotion by saying something like, "John, I sense that you're upset by what I've just said" or words to that effect. Ignoring the emotion and not dealing with it, then and there, will add to their frustration and eventually lead to a breakdown in communications. The white elephant in the room must never be ignored.

That sigh, the crossing of arms along with a look of annoyance and a number of other cues will be your clue to slow things down and deal with what just arose before taking another step along the PIER™. Anchor the emotion instead. Confront the white elephant; but do so gently. It's an elephant after all, and elephants can crush you if not handled gently. By doing this, you're validating the emotion your negotiatee is suddenly feeling, and you're demonstrating empathy. Doing so brings you one step closer to the lighthouse. Doing so shows you care.

Imagine yourself with your partner or with an upset child. If you choose not to identify an emotion that's arisen, the likeliness of that emotion simply going away is quite rare. Ignoring it shuts down and tunes out effective communication. The person you're dealing with stops listening and focuses on the emotion that just crept in – their white elephant. Their dominant thought will be on that emotion or unmet need and quite possibly on your failure to acknowledge it. You don't want their dominant thought to be an unaddressed concern during your negotiation, so it's imperative you address their emotion before moving on.

By identifying and addressing their emotion, you're demonstrating to the other individual that you're listening and that you're prepared to work through their concerns. The moment that you've demonstrated that you truly understand their feelings, their mental attitude will change, and behavioral change then becomes probable. The white elephant feels acknowledged and trusts you'll work through everything with the one they dropped in on, and they'll leave.

Remember to identify the emotion, slow things down and acknowledge their feelings. Only then can a breakthrough happen, and you can then move forward with your negotiation. Anchoring the emotion provides you with an opportunity to dissect it and eliminate it quickly.

Emotion vs. decision-based negotiations: there is a difference worth understanding

As you prepare for your negotiation, understanding the difference between emotion vs. decision-based negotiations is imperative. By now you know you can't control your negotiatee, whoever that may be, but you can control to a greater degree your own emotions. You can – and should keep your emotions under check and develop yellow or red flag alerts that help you to slow things down when the situation calls for it and think intelligently and rationally should you feel pressured or uncertain at any time in the negotiation.

These alert flags are simply awareness triggers to what might not be going so well for you in the negotiation. They will help you to base your decisions not on the emotion of the moment, but on what's fair and right for you while simultaneously understanding that emotion will play a role in every good negotiation.

Again, focus on what you can control: the process and yourself. You can't control the outcome; don't focus on it at first. If closing this deal is your vision, your goal or tunneled vision, then you're focusing on what you can't control, and not on what you can control. Your intent will be misdirected. When you're negotiating with real pros, you'll pay in the end for this misguided approach. So just forget about winning for the moment. That comes later. Focus more on effective decision-making - on being present and alert throughout – on the process instead of the outcome. If you do, you will have a far better chance of achieving your desired outcome with both eyes wide open.

Many people enter a business negotiation *looking for* business solidarity. They look for trust, likeability, connection and the right solution, of course. If you approach a negotiation from the very moment you connect with the mindset that it will be a valuable exchange, as you would with anyone you're trying to impress or influence, then you'll be positively communicating a message of trust and likeability to the other through body language, tone of voice and by the very words you use.

Understanding the 'ins and outs' of emotion and decision-based negotiations

Most people make decisions based on emotion. But that's not how you want either of you to reach agreements on. As much as emotion plays a part in most, if not all of your negotiations, emotion should never be what you base your decisions on, nor should it be what your negotiatees base their decisions on either. As previously discussed, many will ignore "facts" and make decisions based on how they feel – on the emotion of the moment and not on sound decision making. It's only later that they realize this when they step back to look at why they made that decision, and then try to justify it in their heads. There is a great deal of emotion that goes into a successful negotiation, yes; but as a successful negotiator, you must remain in control of your emotions so that you don't overlook the key components in making *sound* decisions.

When you get down to the real negotiation, you're going to want to stir up some calculated emotion in them as well as in yourself, certainly. But never drop your guard or lose your focus. If your negotiatee hits you with a 'Maybe,' don't be either discouraged *or* encouraged by it. Listen to the word. What does 'Maybe' really mean? It's neither a "No" nor a "Yes." It's a 'Maybe.' Your job will be to find out what it is that is keeping it a "Maybe." Asking the right questions will work in this situation - questions such as, "Is there anything that I haven't covered that worries you?"

One of my favorite approaches, when a person has left me wondering, has been to repeat two or three of the last words they uttered in question form. I've mentioned this, but it is worth repeating. For example, using the approach in the examples I provided earlier, should the other negotiator come up with a "Maybe," you simply repeat that last word as a question. "Maybe...?" Use a soft, inquisitive voice. And if they follow up with a sentence that still has you baffled, do it again: repeat ono to three of their last words. (Think 1-2-3 next time you need more information).

> **Client**: "I'll have to consider this. All I can say at the moment is maybe."
>
> **You**: "Maybe...?" (A one-word prompt).
>
> **Client**: "Yeah, I'll have to run it by a few people."
>
> **You**: "A few people?" (A three-word prompt).
>
> **Client**: "Yeah, we have a board we have to run things by. They make all the final decisions."
>
> **You**: "Sure, I understand that. Makes perfect sense. John, is there anything I haven't covered or satisfied you of that worries you or that you feel your board may need to hear more about to help you, and them reach a decision? I'm confident I can provide all of you with whatever clarification you need."

Notice how simply asking a one to three-word, open-ended question elicits more information? I used it effectively in most of my interrogations and negotiations. "Maybe" is not what you're looking for in any negotiation. Deal with it then and there. You're looking for a 'Yes.' When you first walk into a negotiation room, it's obviously a 'No' or you're at ground zero. That's an excellent place to start.

Be cautious of a "Yes" too quickly, in a business negotiation especially. When that happens, it's quite often followed by a "But," "When" or "If." And that means they likely want you to give in a little more – or a lot more. They expect you to make concessions - to take a cut. Be careful of a *yes* too quickly.

For the reasons noted above, reaching a 'yes' too soon can cause you to become unfocused and too emotional, leading you to imagine that the deal is done. It will hurt when you later discover that the 'yes' you received so quickly was not unconditional. If your negotiatee leads right off the bat with a "Yes," then your job will be to explore every meaning of what that "Yes" involves. Don't get too excited. Simply make sure that you're both in agreement on every point being negotiated, and by doing so, you may discover that there are a few points that still need to be negotiated.

Does a fast "Yes" ever happen with a positive, unfettered outcome? It does. It happens when your negotiatee has done his or her homework on you and believes in everything that you can provide. It happens if they've negotiated with you before and were happy with the results. There are a number of reasons why someone may choose to reach a "Yes" from the very onset, but if you've never negotiated with this negotiatee before, be cautious of it. My earlier example involving a workshop in Lisbon, Portugal is an excellent example of how a 'yes' can be reached almost immediately.

The "Maybe" is not a "No" – it's a stepping stone which means they're just not ready to commit just yet and there's more to discuss. At least with a "Maybe" you know that the person sitting across from you is considering your offer and is prepared to discuss things further and rationally. And is that not why you're there in the first place - to discuss rationally and to negotiate fairly? One of the things to remember is that "Maybe" and "No" get you and your negotiatee discussing the things that matter to both of you. If at some point you feel your negotiatee is asking for too much – things you aren't willing (or shouldn't) give, invite your negotiatee to say "No," or say so yourself.

Let's face it, some companies and clients will ask for far too much. And if you give in simply to reach a "Yes," the consequences of doing so will undoubtedly come back to haunt you. More so, it will leave your negotiatee thinking less of you while having acquired more from you. Who loses then? Remember that you didn't enter the negotiation room to be taken advantage of or to give in to too much.

In business, for example, what you're offering is value and services for a fair price. You entered that negotiation room knowing what you needed and wanted, understanding that the negotiation starts with a "No" and being prepared to negotiate fairly to reach a 'Yes' you can both live with. Stick to the plan.

If your potential client is asking you for too much, be it time, service or product that is not profitable for you to give with what the offer is on the table, say so. Say something like, "Bob, I understand what you're asking for, but I just can't give it to you. If I do, I'll be left with no profit whatsoever, and I want to have this work out for each of us. Let's see what more we can work on together." Doing so will not kill the deal for you.

Remember that this is a professional discussion. If you got this far with your negotiatee, they're interested in what you have to offer. They may hesitate at first while they consider your proposal, but it doesn't necessarily mean it's a no. And if it's you who have turned away because you weren't willing to give that much, then you've won. Don't be surprised if they call you back to go ahead with the deal. Providing you were professional, confident and friendly.

As a successful negotiator, you must remain in control of your own emotions so that you don't overlook the key components in making sound decisions.

There is a lot of power in the word "No." I used it often myself in hostage and in crisis negotiations. You can well imagine the demands that a hostage taker might make during the crisis: demands for liquor, drugs, prostitutes, safe passage out, a plane, a million bucks and so forth. I could never give a "Yes" or a "Maybe" to such demands. Answers like these were not in my best interests, nor were they in the best interests of the hostages or the public. A calm "*No*" followed by, "That's something I just can't do, Mike," or, "How am I supposed to do that, Bill?" didn't close the negotiation. It simply led to what *I could do* for them and took the focus off what I *couldn't* do for them - value as opposed to consequence. And that's how it should be in your business and life negotiations.

As you can see, there is some work you must do during preparation before you engage with your negotiatee. Planning is imperative. Before we go on to **Intent**, let me recap what we've covered so far in this chapter:

Planning - Key Points:

- Preparing for the negotiation, the meeting, the interview, a date and whatever else it is you're after, is vitally important to your chances of success.

- Self-evaluation involves taking a deep and focused look at our weaknesses and our self-sabotaging beliefs, and should we uncover the beasts, on working on ridding ourselves of them.

- History has taught us that focusing on the *self* first was ineffective in hostage negotiations. It resulted in the loss of life. Using a more emotion-based and 'take your time' approach in dealing with others has proven to be more successful.

- You have the power of turning your fear into courage. You have the power of choosing positive self-talk over negative self-talk.

- In life and when meeting someone new, don't try to be perfect. Remember that the person you're negotiating with is just like you. A human being living a human and often un-perfect existence. They trip up, drop stuff, miss cues and experience just about everything you do.

- We all suffer from self-doubt at some point. Deal with any self-doubt in the planning phase. You mustn't allow a past failure, or a fear of failure, comparison or judgement prevent you from moving ahead in negotiations and in life.

- Knowing your value and knowing when to move forward and when to walk away from any negotiation or life interaction makes you a winner. Undercutting yourself devalues you, and you end up losing, no matter what you're after. Without developing a confidence-to-negotiate or to ask for what you want in life, you'll fail to achieve the results you seek.

- Sincerity and credibility comes out in our voice and our body language, and if our motives for asking are in any way insincere, the other person will instinctively pick up on it.

- Being aware that you have a right to ask for what you want once you've established the groundwork and followed the steps to do so is a liberating truth.

- Build a bridge and take down the wall. We all instinctively have walls to keep us protective from possible harm. Our job as negotiators and people seeking to get more out of life is to break down the walls and build bridges.

- Role-playing pre-negotiation can help to prepare you for whatever comes your way. Anticipate every question that may be asked of you and prepare your answers. If you're lucky enough to be working with a partner, each of you takes on a role: one as the negotiator from your company and the other as the negotiator from theirs. Have fun with it and then switch it up and reverse roles.

- Imagine the many questions that may be asked of you during the negotiation and be prepared to answer each and every one of them. Be prepared for the unexpected and if you don't have an answer, assure them that you will find one for them and deliver on what you promise.

- Get over fear. Remember that this is an opportunity for both of you.

- Once you understand who you're negotiating with, consider how you'll dress for the meeting. When in doubt: Just ask.

- Be confident. Remember that a positive self-image is one of the keys to success.

- Find out as much as you can about who you will be negotiating with – *and* who your competition is. Doing so provides you a sense of who they are and what they value.

- One of the most important keys to your success in life and in business negotiations is being honest. Fool now, and you'll be the fool later. If you aren't the right match for that business, that person, that job – admit it and move on.

- Before you negotiate, be aware that there are both internal and external factors at play in every negotiation. We can control the internal factors as they are within ourselves; they are our moods, our words, our body gestures and our intentions, to mention but a few. But we can't control the external factors as they are NOT within ourselves – but in the person we're interacting with.

- Time is one of a negotiator's greatest tools. Whenever possible, take the time you need to get the job done right. Never feel rushed or create a sense of urgency in yourself, or your negotiatee. Doing so will force you to take shortcuts. If you need more time, ask for it.

- Most of us make decisions based on emotion. Many people will ignore "facts" and make decisions based on how they feel – on their emotion at the time. There is a great deal of emotion that goes into a successful negotiation; but as a successful negotiator, you must remain aware of your own emotions so that you don't overlook the key components in making sound decisions.

- Saying 'no' is everybody's right, including yours. 'No' is where most negotiations begin. Never fear the word 'no' – it's simply a starting point. It will be up to you to turn that 'no' into a 'yes' using the methods and principles found here.

Call to Action:

- This one will be fun. Whatever you have coming up next, practice for it first by role-playing with a partner. Do you have a business negotiation planned? Get someone to play the role of your negotiatee and have

143

them ask you the tough questions. Have your answers prepared so well that they will not sound scripted. Switch roles partway through and do it until it's easy. Have fun.

Let's now move ahead to the **I** in PIER™: **Intent**

Chapter Four

———•◆◆◆•———

PRINCIPLE NUMBER 2: INTENT

The 'I' in PIER™ Negotiating - Intent

The previous chapter on **Planning** examined not only the importance of preparation and preparedness, but also examined the importance of strategizing and of conducting periodic and necessary self-examinations. It also laid out the importance of understanding your value and self-worth, while considering the self-worth and value of those you will be interacting with on your road to reaching agreements. Everyone has a right to say 'No' – including you. 'Role-playing' can not only get you ready to work a room confidently, it's also fun. Researching who you'll be meeting and negotiating with gives you an advantage you otherwise would not have had.

Take a few minutes prior to any negotiation and do your utmost best to know as much about who you'll be negotiating with as you can. In life negotiations that may not always be possible – but you should never overlook trying. The internet may uncover some amazing information.

> "Our intention creates our reality."
> **Wayne Dyre**

This reminds me of a wonderful woman I dated a couple of years back. We'd met online and we were talking about our online experiences one evening. She told me of a man she'd dated for a couple of months. He seemed nice in the beginning, but was very evasive when it came to answering questions about his ex and children. The more she inquired, the more he came up with different stories – a web of lies and deceit as she later discovered.

She eventually decided to search him on the Internet. What took her so long she couldn't say. Much to her astonishment, she discovered that he was an ax murderer. Yep. No kidding. True story. To make matters worse, he'd killed his wife with an ax, had served a lengthy prison sentence and had just been released. He only got caught because he involved a friend to help hide the body. What's that joke about a true friend is one who helps you move the body? Obviously, his friend wasn't *that* friend and called the cops. I remembered that case because I was a detective at the time he'd axed his wife to death and it occurred in one of our jurisdictions, although I was not assigned to the case. Thankfully, that story had a happy ending. She ran and kept her head about it.

How intention works

Intention cannot be seen. It can only be felt and experienced through associated behavior. Intention is a representation of the motives and attitudes *behind* the actions. Even if you have the best intentions in mind, it will mean absolutely nothing unless you express those intentions clearly through your behavior. Intention and behavior must work together in lock-step, otherwise the imbalance will be obvious, and your *negotiation* will become no more than an average business transaction.

If you drop *intent* from PIER™ negotiating, you will not get the best results you could have otherwise achieved by keeping this vital principle where it belongs. Imagine overlooking a key ingredient to one of your favorite recipes – it just won't turn out as good as it could. I want you to link *intent* with *meaningful behavior* because intent without meaningful behavior means nothing at all. It would be like telling someone you love them and doing nothing after that to show it. You leave the recipient of that 'I love you' wondering, "Does he/she?" Intent and meaningful behavior must be in balance, like the image of the Ying and the Yang.

No matter what you're after in life, whether you're planning to ask for a job, a better position within your organization, a break on rent, a discount at a boutique you're shopping in, agreements from a client or whether you wish to help your negotiatee succeed, not only must you plan ahead, engage to make the very best first impression you possibly can and build a relationship, you must do so using the principle of *meaningful intention*. Having the right intention begins in the mind and results in behavior.

People will not judge you on your good intentions alone; they will additionally judge you on your behavior. They cannot *see* your intentions. You must communicate them clearly, and you do so through your spoken word followed by the action you promise.

We don't judge people on their intentions alone, do we? We judge them by what they do and whether they're as good as their word. We can't read anyone's mind, but we sure can read their behavior. If someone tells us they'll be somewhere at a certain time to meet us for the first time, and they don't show up on time, it affects how we see them. We wonder if this is their habit and whether they'll do it to us again next time. Even if they tell us, "Hey, I had every intention of getting here on time, but I got caught up in traffic. Sorry." That doesn't do much to assure us of their reliability, does it? We may think, "It's midday, of course traffic will be heavy! Why didn't you leave earlier? My time is valuable, and you didn't consider traffic?! Don't you value my time?"

Now you may be thinking, "Paul, that happens. Why are you being so mean?" I'm not. It's the way most of us think. We could care less about excuses. Think of a time where someone promised to pay you what they owed you by a certain date, or a contractor called at the last minute to tell you they couldn't get to your place for another few hours or few days, or showed up late. Or a service provider about to install your internet service and didn't show up. Did you

> Intention is a representation of the motives and attitudes behind the actions. Even if you have the best intentions in mind, it will mean absolutely nothing unless you express those intentions clearly through your behavior.

really care about their so-called good intentions? I'm going to suggest "hell, no!", most of us don't give a damn. We care about results: delivery on promises. We want to trust their word.

We put weight into what people tell us and we judge them by what they do. We weigh whether their word matches their actions. They do the same of you. In the example I gave you earlier about the traffic delay, I agree that there will be times in which delays will be unavoidable, no matter how well ahead you've planned. These are the exceptions, and occasionally in cases like this, whoever you're meeting will hear about it on the news or through someone else. But a first meeting? A first date? Really?

We're more likely to forgive someone when we know they did their absolute best to deliver on their word. That's why we should never promise anything we may not be able to deliver on. Our intent must be sincere and focused on the one we're dealing with: our clients, children, bosses, partners, employees and so forth, followed by the behaviors our intent meant to supply, otherwise we may fall short of delivering on what we promised, and we may be perceived as an unreliable fraud. This applies to business negotiations as much as it does to life negotiations.

We cannot leave our intent to chance. It's not like we can simply meet someone, promise them the world and leave making up our intent later along the way. That just won't do. Doing so misses the principle of planning completely. We must take control of our intent. Yes, intent is a big part of preparation. Remember that each step of the PIER™ is vitally important if you are to get what you want in life.

***

Your good intentions cannot be seen. To show them off, you must demonstrate them through your behavior. Only then can they be felt and experienced by others.

***

Guidepost number four: Demonstrate intent through word and action

If I tell you I love you and don't show it through my words and behavior, or tell you I'll do something and fail to do it, I've not only broken my word, I've let you down. That is unacceptable in PIER™ negotiating on all levels: life and business. Good intentions begin in the mind and must be demonstrated more explicitly through action. The right intent begins in the mind and results in behavior.

If we focus only on ourselves and overlook the wonderful opportunity to have respectful and meaningful moments with those we negotiate with—be it in life or in business —we jeopardize our chances of long-term success. When we approach our

> **Good intentions begin in the mind and are revealed more explicitly through action.**

negotiation with the right intent, and take the time to nurture the relationship (the behavior behind the intent), our chances of success expand tremendously. Doing so allows for our specific goal-oriented successes to become more accessible.

How we communicate our good intentions

By now you know that we communicate your good intentions in two ways: verbally and through behavior. People can't read our minds but they can certainly read our behavior. And they sure as heck will.

I'm an advocate of verbalizing intention. It's amazing how by verbalizing something can help make it so. But do so only if you have honestly evaluated yourself and know that your word **is** your bond. If it is, say so. Tell your negotiatee what you are committed to doing. Write it down if that helps. You may need to do so in the contract after all, but how about just writing it down right in front of them or in a journal as a promise to yourself?

Business Bulletin # 9: The business client's point of view - on you

Let's get back to the business negotiation for a moment. If you have your negotiatees' best interests in mind and have verbalized that you do and/or have begun to show them that you do, you're on your way to establishing trust and building rapport, preludes to the relationship.

Once your negotiatee feels that your intent is in their genuine interests, they will be more likely to tell you what they think, feel and hope to accomplish with you. Be honest about your intent and should there be a time during your negotiation where you encounter hesitation or resistance, be prepared to re-vocalize what your intent is and get them talking about their concerns.

For example, you may wish to assure your client verbally that you intend to help them be more successful with their business whether they choose to work with you or not. You may wish to tell them that you intend to help them make the best choice for themselves and to feel assured that what you have to offer is a good fit for them.

Keep this in mind: you will broadcast your intent in one (or all) of three ways: verbally (through the spoken word), nonverbally (through your body language) and by the tone of your voice. Our primal selves provide us with the ability to discern whether or not the person we're engaging with is a threat or someone we can trust. The promising words you say will definitely be nice to hear, but they must also be consistent with your actions. One way or another, your intent will come through. You'll only prove your intent through the associated behavior.

You're always being assessed

The person sitting across from you is in constant assessment mode. They're watching your every move and evaluating whether or not your words are congruent with your body language and the tone of your voice. They're watching your face for changes in expression; they're watching your body language and evaluating when it changes; they're listening to the tone of your voice to evaluate truth. They may be doing this instinctively or consciously. Therefore, all three communication modes (words, tone and body language) must be working simultaneously – in sync, when you're delivering your message or proposal. As I said earlier, you must be aware of your own body language as much as you are of theirs. Watch for indicators that project uncertainty or confusion, both in you and your negotiatee. Then address them.

For you, watch for things as subtle as leaning away from them, rubbing your hands, shifting your eyes away from theirs, and a multitude of other indicators. Your body language will affect your negotiatee, positively or negatively. In all cases, your intention will in part be conveyed through your body language, and it will affect both you and your negotiatee. It will set the mood and affect the outcome. Never ignore nonverbal messages or cues that you become aware of in the negotiation (the white elephants). Identify them, call them out *softly* for what they appear to be and take the necessary steps to address them completely before moving forward. Never ignore them.

What are your negotiatee's intentions?

So now you get the importance of intention and you're preparing to meet your negotiatee. In the prep phase, you did your due diligence and checked up on them, as best you could, and depending on what was available, gathered whatever helpful information you could that might help you as you move nicely into the negotiation. Maybe you discovered they're an ax murderer and cancelled the meet. Damn good for you! You just never know, and that's why doing your absolute best to find out as much as you can about them is so vitally important. I'm glad my friend Chris did, otherwise I may never have met her.

So next, you'll want to consider "Who am I going to be negotiating with?", "What are *their* intentions?", and "How do I create an environment of trust, likeability, and cooperation to successfully bring this to a positive outcome?" to name but a few considerations.

I understood the importance of bringing my "best me" to the negotiation and leaving whatever noise I didn't need behind. Noise is whatever is holding you back from having a clear, focused mind and client-based or people-based approach. Dramas we may be experiencing in our personal or professional lives, deadlines, other meetings and an array of 'others' focus robbers have no place occupying our thoughts during any negotiation. That's 'noise,' and it interferes with your objective: providing your negotiatee your undivided attention. Whatever noise you may have floating around in your thought's pre-negotiation must be left at the door before you enter into any negotiation. You can pick them up once you're done, if you so choose.

Trust yourself and bring what you know to the negotiation with the utmost confidence and right intent, so that it will then paint a perfect balance of verbal and non-verbal influence for your negotiatee. Without doing so, you may be setting myself up to fail. Knowing your product and services inside and out, having prepared and role-played for whatever questions, concerns and/or objections might come your way is extremely important to your overall success. As is having the right intent. Later, you'll have them reciprocating what you give.

The negotiation would be meaningless, one-sided and incomplete without the *honest* and open input of your negotiatee. Real people sit across from you during your negotiation, and they have their own concerns, needs, and expectations. As do you. They need to know that your intent is in both your mutual interests, and this is why taking a moment to consider their intentions pre-negotiation makes sense. You may find the following list helpful for doing so.

Checklist considerations:

- What is my intention in this negotiation/interaction?

- What is my "budget"? (In both business or personal negotiations involving costs)

- Keep your objectives and intentions in mind and listen first.

- Consider the other person's POV – Point of View.

- Who am I negotiating with?

- What are their objectives/intentions?

- How do I create an environment of trust, likeability and cooperation?

- Plan whenever possible. Practice whenever possible. Be prepared for objections and have an answer ready. I.e., "I understand your concerns, John. I want you to know that I'm committed to helping you avoid any difficulty in the future. I have a plan…"

- Speak their language. Be willing and able to adapt to their style, i.e., nuances and cultural implications behind what is being said. Ask for clarification whenever needed. By taking the time to understand the other party's history, culture, and perspective, you send the message that you're committed to the negotiation and the relationship—an integral step in trust building. Ask for clarification whenever a particular word comes up that may have a different meaning to them. Understand what they mean by a particular term that comes out during the negotiation. Ask.

- In a business negotiation, state at the outset of the negotiation that you have worked and will continue to work to understand their perspective, needs and interests, and that you recognize—and hope that they do, too—that a lot of learning will take place as the negotiation moves forward and the relationship builds. Express the hope that when a mistake or misunderstanding occurs, as some inevitably will, both sides will see it as a natural part of the learning process and redouble efforts to reach an understanding of the other's point of view.

- Manage your reputation. In negotiation, as in all aspects of life, your reputation often precedes you. A bad reputation can be a deal killer from the start, while a great one can help transcend an impasse. Effective negotiators realize that their reputation is not just a backdrop, but a tool. How can you make your reputation a factor in negotiation? You might provide references from mutually trusted third parties that vouch for your character and competence.

- Don't make dependence a factor. The more dependent you are on someone, the more willing you'll be to trust them and do whatever they say. Remember that neediness has no place in any negotiation. This phenomenon plays out to the extreme in the Stockholm syndrome, in which hostages become so psychologically dependent on their captors that they'll trust their captors' statements and demands more than those of the officials who are attempting to negotiate their release…

- We tend to cope with the psychological discomfort associated with dependence by believing in the trustworthiness of those upon whom we depend. In negotiation, when both parties believe that they need each other to achieve their individual goals and that other options are limited, trust between parties will increase. As a negotiator, you can trigger this trust-building process by highlighting the unique benefits you can provide and by emphasizing the damage that might result from an impasse.

Negotiations with strangers and enemies who have no interest in the other tend to be calculative, with both parties carefully measuring what they're gaining with each concession made by the other side. By contrast, negotiations based on long-term relationships are usually less focused on tallying up wins and losses. A carefully crafted unilateral concession can work wonders for trust, for it conveys to the other party that you consider the relationship to be a friendly one, with the potential for mutual gain and trust over time.

Again, a big part of success comes from understanding that the person being negotiated with is just *like you*. Put yourself in their shoes and choose your **language** carefully. What do I mean by language? Words, tone and body. Consider:

- **Words**: Use their language, your delivery. Professional, focused, inquisitive, purposeful, directed – know when to talk and when to listen

- **Tone**: Confident, controlled and free from uncertainty. The correct pitch in your voice.

- **Body language**: Be aware of yours and theirs. People will judge you in the first $1/10^{th}$ of a second, give or take. First impressions last a long time. Make yours matter positively. The smile, the professional handshake, your confidence, how you're dressed, your tone of voice… they all matter. What is their body language telling you? How was their handshake? Their smile? The way they carried themselves?

Take mental snapshots throughout your negotiation. Look for changes in body language when a different issue is discussed. Are they showing more interest? Less interest? Anger? Fear? Concern? Address the emotion whenever needed. Don't avoid it. That helps builds trust.

Walls can pop up in any interaction and negotiation. One of the keys to tearing down walls is to recognize they exist. Once you recognize them, you're less likely to run full speed into them. You stop, pause a moment and address them. You listen to the wall builder – get their point of view. Then you work at tearing the walls down with the intent of building bridges. One approach may simply be to ask for *their* solution first: "How would you go about...?"

The 'new generation' of potential negotiators/adversaries may have a slightly different language and/or point of view. Understand it's from *their* point of view and work with it while maintaining your objectives. It's a partnership after all.

Many negotiators mistakenly focus on the end first, with no genuine negotiatee-focused intent. The outcome is something you can't control. Focus on the means rather. By doing that, you'll have a greater chance of an excellent outcome. Forget about closing the deal. Concentrate on the journey - the interaction; the relationship; understanding of the person's needs and concerns and on making sound judgments.

Recovering from negotiation break down

It might just happen. You're human, after all. What if you do make a mistake? Is it the end of the world? No, it's not. If for example, a business negotiation came to an abrupt halt as a result of a misunderstanding or miscommunication either through you or anyone else on your team, re-group, re-plan and ask to re-negotiate. Yes, ask to re-negotiate.

Many negotiators and business professionals believe that if they blew it the first time, the game's over. Not necessarily. It depends on the circumstances and how important the negotiation is to *all* stakeholders.

Most everything can be salvaged – especially if you established yourself as professional, trustworthy and respectful from the onset. *Ask* for a second chance and then rehearse (role-play) until you get it right for your second time around. You may or may not be granted another opportunity, but just ask anyway.

The same holds true in your life negotiations. If something went wrong, step back, assess the reality of the situation, and decide if it's worth going after again. Chances are it will be; asking for a second chance is fine unless you really messed up. Even a third time – if timed right, and again – depending on the circumstances.

Most business professionals will stop asking after the second request, but in life matters, relationships in particular, some of us ask more than twice, which is not always the best thing to do. Especially if you've done your very best on the previous occasions you've asked.

Consider whether asking for that third 'shot' will make you look like you're evolving into a stalker (or business pest if you decided to try for number three), or if it makes you look too needy. If you time it correctly, that third request for consideration may be welcomed – in business and in life. If it is your third time around, don't chase the moment – let the moment come to you.

> **Don't focus on the end results. Know what you want, yes, but focus instead on what you can control - the means, and not on what is not within your control: the end result.**

In business for example, if you blew it, give it a few days to settle, and when you're ready to fix it, make the call. If it's a no, consider trying some time down the road when the memory of what went wrong may not be so strong, **and only** if and when the opportunity presents itself – not you hunting it down. In life matters, try the same. Timing is extremely important. You don't want to project neediness after all.

Should your negotiation break down, show the negotiatee that you're only human, just like them, and that you're prepared to admit you made an error and work with them from there. There's nothing wrong in apologizing. Don't let ego get the best of you. There are a million reasons you might get rejected, so never take it personally if you know you did nothing wrong but do have a backup plan. For us as hostage negotiators, that was having a secondary negotiator, for one.

***

There is no shame in apologizing if and when you mess things up. In fact, a sincere apology will go a long way in mending a damaged bridge.

***

Bad decisions and how to recover from them

We all screw up from time to time, but the important thing is to learn from each muck up so as to minimize the chance of repeating it a second or third time. God knows I've had my share, and each time, I forgive myself for it, learn from it and move the hell along. Life teaches us many lessons as Bruce Lee pointed out, but only if we're students of life *willing* to be taught. See failures as lessons that may sting the face when they hit you - and grow from them. Be aware that you're human and as such, that all humans are imperfect. Don't beat the hell out of yourself for having made it. Learn, forgive but don't forget. Move on.

We are imperfect people living in an imperfect world. But what we have going for us is the ability to change and to create different outcomes and successes for ourselves, despite what happens. Once we learn from the mistakes we've made in the past and appreciate them as life lessons, we're not as likely to repeat those mistakes. Unless we're hard-headed, narrow-minded idiot asses suffering from tunnel vision, that is.

Only a fool chooses to make the same mistakes over and over, and you're no fool. Albert Einstein once said: "The definition of insanity is doing the same thing over and over again while expecting different results." If you leave the negotiation, be it in life or in business with the realization that you've made a mistake, don't kick yourself stupid for it. Think about it, dissect it, learn from it and look at it as being handed a gift. Yes, a gift. It's really up to you whether or not you want to see it as a gift or not, but I recommend that you do. And if you do, unwrap it carefully and examine everything: the bow, the paper, and the contents. Dissect the damn thing. This will help you learn from it, prepare you to make whatever adjustments necessary and keep you from repeating the same mistake twice. It's the school of hard knocks we learn the most from in life, baby, and sometimes mistakes are unfortunately made. Get over them.

Learning from your mistakes helps you reach perfection. And if the error was not unfixable and you feel you have an opening to go back to your negotiatee and explain yourself while asking for another shot, do it. They'll appreciate your honesty and your integrity for doing so. Most successful people in life are the ones who made mistakes – plenty of them – but modified their approach and learned from them. They weren't afraid to ask for another chance. They weren't afraid to try again.

Failure can be one of your best teachers

If a negotiation goes to shit, consider doing the following:

- Acknowledge the breakdown that occurred and take accountability and responsibility for it (especially if it was with you that it broke down) without losing your credibility as a new negotiator, should this be the case as it was in my story.

- Don't let your ego get the best of you.

- Start afresh by stating what your desired outcome is (your intent) and that you're prepared to work with that person to help you both reach an agreeable outcome, together.

- Focus on what went well in the earlier negotiation.

- If time has passed between the first negotiation and the second negotiation, you have time to research the reasons why the negotiation broke down. Pick whatever points you can from that experience and rehearse how you'll address it.

- Learn from what went wrong and don't be afraid to embark on a new negotiation with the individual. In hostage negotiations, we have no choice. Try at least one more time – in all negotiation scenarios, but don't try so often you become a deal stalker.

Your intent will come through. If you're second at the bat, project a sincere intent to fix what went wrong with your first negotiator and work at finding solutions together.

We all know that from time to time negotiations or relationships within our homes or offices do break down. I don't know of any negotiator who doesn't experience that on occasion – a negotiation that doesn't always work out in their favor. Being prepared to handle what happens next is crucial. If you find yourself in a situation where the negotiation has fallen off the rails, be ready to re-examine whether it's worth taking a second shot at it. Most often, it is.

Equals in negotiation

While on the topic of being human, is anyone better than the other? Nope. You're equals. Being an equal in any negotiation is an absolute must. As I touched on briefly in Chapter two, being an equal in the negotiation sets a good tone for you and your negotiatee, one of respect, and ensures you won't be seen as needy and weak. There should be 'no top dog' in the negotiation as you recall. This does not only apply to business – it applies in life as well.

Here's what to do to personalize and equalize the negotiation right from the start. If you choose to give your negotiatee a title, for example, 'Mister Jones,' 'Doctor Smith', 'Mayor Bob' or whatever, you're left with a disadvantage from the very beginning. The title you give or leave attached to them gives them power. For example, consider this simple exchange:
Negotiatee: "Hi, I'm Joseph Smith."
Negotiator: "Hello Mister Smith."

Not dropping the title, whenever possible, creates an imbalance between the negotiator and negotiatee. In this example, Joseph Smith is going to feel like he's the top dog in the room. His status just got higher than his negotiatee because he was given permission to feel that way. He's going to feel like he has an advantage over his negotiatee right from the very beginning.

Consider this instead:
Your negotiatee: "Hi, I'm Joseph Smith."

You: (To illustrate, I'll use my own name in this example.) "Hi Joseph. I'm Paul Nadeau. Just call me Paul. Nice to finally meet you." (First and last name to begin).

With a few carefully selected simple words, you've leveled the playing field and have subtly established that you are equals from the start. It also helps to build rapport by using their first names throughout, so once the initial introduction has been made, you'll go on to using first names - and no titles. Everybody loves the sound of their name. It helps put you on the road to establishing a good connection.

The title 'Mr.' or 'Mrs.' has an effect. As I said, in most cases, drop it. I say "in most cases" because occasionally you'll encounter legitimate exceptions where dropping the title will be a sign of disrespect. For example, if you happened to be addressing someone of high social or political status... you wouldn't refer to them by their first names... especially if you want to build a good and lasting relationship with them. It would be seen as a sign of disrespect. And nothing will destroy a relationship faster than disrespect.

As I mentioned, I also used this successfully in the interrogations of all suspects I dealt with. I would walk into the room, greet them by using my first and last name, asking them to call me by my first and then asking them for theirs. I would also make sure to ask what they wanted to be called. Not only to get the pronunciation correct but also to determine what they preferred to be called. I'd ask: "What do you like to be called?" I would never assume. For example, John may not appreciate it if you were to call him "Johnny."

Exploring 'wants and legitimate needs' in you and others

As you prepare for your business or life negotiation, be conscious of what you tell and convince yourself of. Create a positive self-monologue in your head and stick to it. Have your bottom line clear before you start. Remember that a deal is just a deal. If you're a goal-oriented force to be reckoned with, losing out on one deal won't be the end of you. You'll do whatever is within your power to get it, recognizing that there is only so much you can control and if this one doesn't work out, you'll make the other one work out. Sometimes it's just not meant to be, and sometimes it turns out for the best. We simply don't know.

You're damn near limitless after all, and you know your value and your self-worth. This you discovered when you evaluated yourself honestly in preparation to move ahead confidently with your negotiation. You understand that you won't always get what you're after; but knowing that won't discourage you from going after everything you want despite that reality. You'll trash the idea of being 'needy' and focus on replacing that notion with a more realistic and manageable concept: that of wanting what you want, not needing what you want.

Just as you have wants and must-haves, so does your negotiatee. They are, after all, just like you. They agreed to meet with you because maybe they want your business, your product or your companionship. They have their lists of wants, and yes, expectations. Maybe they're unrealistic, but they have them nevertheless, as do you. Knowing that they have wants, you'll work at determining what those wants and expectations are through exploratory dialogue.

You'll do so not to take advantage of them, but to understand them, and to determine if what you or your company have to offer (or on life matters – whether **you**) are a good fit for them. After all, in order to reach an agreement that will be mutually beneficial for each of you, you do want to supply them with as close to what they want and need as possible, if not bang on. We know that it might not be exactly what they'd pictured at first, because some of our negotiatees don't even know exactly what they want, as we now understand.

And that's why you're there. To hear them out, help them out and once all the facts are in, to propose the best solution you have to offer that will meet their interests. You'll have explored what those interests and desires exhaustively – and in business negotiations, by understanding needs and wants through deliberate exploratory dialogue, you may just find excellent opportunities to offer your negotiatee services and/or products they'd not considered in the first place (remember the Prince story?) Bonus!

Some of you are likely shaking your head right now and saying, "Paul, in business we often *need!*" I agree. That product or service may, in fact, be something you or they need to make it all work, but please understand the concept of what I'm setting out here: I'm referring primarily to emotional neediness and misguided attachment longing.

If it's a part, a widget, a service or product that makes the whole thing work, that's clearly different. Legitimate needs do absolutely exist. We address them as passionately as every other step of our negotiation. What I'm saying is not a contradiction – it's working with whatever the reality of the situation is, and being able to adapt to the situation, no matter what it may be; and to keep a level and professional head about it.

By now some of you may also be asking, "Is this not exactly what you just told us to avoid? Are we not sharks if we try to expose their wants and needs?" The answer to that question is 'no, you are not.' The answer lies in your "intent." Comparatively, a shark wants to expose your weaknesses and the neediness of the ones across from them so that they can *take advantage* of them. But in your case, as a fair, well-intentioned and professional negotiator, you must expose their wants (and yes, needs) to see if you *can* provide solutions for them and to see if you're a fit for them, and them for you - not take them for everything they've got.

Creating a genuine want or solution for your negotiatee

Creating a want – or a solution - in your negotiatee for your services or what you have to offer (by asking the right kinds of questions and encouraging the right kind of emotion to surface) makes perfect sense, providing what you have **is** right for them. Create a well-intentioned, legitimate need - a solution - for them, and they'll want to deal with you. This is one of the keys to successful negotiations.

> People want to leave that negotiating feeling that they were heard, appreciated and that they had their needs met with what was right for them, whether or not some small concessions were made to get there.

At the end of the day, we all want to feel okay with ourselves and with the decisions we've made. We all want the other person sitting across from us to feel okay with us, and their decisions too. We all sleep better that way. And so it is with negotiations. People want to leave that negotiating feeling that they were heard, appreciated and that they had their needs met with what was right for them, whether or not some small concessions were made along the way. They want to feel like they've made the right decision.

Although you don't show yourself as a needy person, it's your job is to bring out their legitimate *neediness* to discover the right solution so you can help solve what they need taken care of with your guidance. This cannot be mistaken with manipulation because it isn't. It's simply discovering the desired outcome need in the other person so that you can address it to their satisfaction, and to yours. Case in point: imagine not creating a need for survival with my hostage takers. I gave them something of value to 'need' and focus on as being the best solution for them. Life over death.

Negotiate the way you would like to be negotiated with

Regardless of race, culture, religious beliefs or backgrounds, we are all more similar than we are different. You're likely thinking, "We get it, dude." Yes, by now, having stuck with me so far, you do. But this is one of those advantage points worth solidifying to memory. Doing so will reward you immensely in business and in life. It's worth repeating, and in this next passage I'll put a spin on it.

We all laugh, love and bleed in the same way. We all have relationships and things of personal importance that matter to us, and we all want to live comfortable, happy and uncomplicated lives. At least most of us do. This is an extremely important key to keep in mind as you negotiate, especially with others who may have different beliefs, backgrounds or points of view that differ from yours.

For me, I negotiated with hostage takers and hardened criminals including murders, rapists and child molesters. Not to mention the odd terrorist. They often did and saw things differently than I. For you, I have no idea with whom you'll be negotiating with or how different your points of view on some matters may be. What I do know is that in order to meet in agreement, we must be willing to separate a persons' actions from who they are whenever it becomes necessary to do so. And it often does. What I mean by this is we mustn't hold what a person has done or said, or what they believe in, against them if we hope to influence their behavior and later get cooperation from them.

We're not always right in our assumptions of others, and we certainly don't always see things the way they do. If we enter into any negotiation with a misguided or incorrect negative pre-determined judgement of the person we'll be negotiating with, our bias or prejudices will show through. We won't be able to hide it.

For instance, if I walked into an interrogation room with the intent of only getting a confession from a murderer and kept what he/she had done in the forefront of my mind, thinking, "You despicable piece of crap!", then somewhere in my words, tone of voice, body language and approach I'd involuntarily (or voluntarily) broadcast that resentment to him/her, and my chances of getting the suspect to cooperate would be slim to none.

On the other hand, when I reminded myself that I was going to be negotiating with someone who, for reasons unknown to me yet, had committed a crime and that I sincerely wanted to understand the motivation behind the act, while reminding myself (and them) that there was still some good left in them, then that intent would be the message they'd receive, helping bridge the trust I needed to get what I wanted. Do you get it? My non-judgement of them would lower their self-preservation guards – their 'walls' - long enough for me to build a foundation on which to move forward. By not keeping what they were suspected of doing in the forefront, I got to connect with the person first – not the criminal. That makes a huge difference. Did that mean that I was okay with what they'd done? Not at all. What it meant was that I wasn't going to enter into the negotiation holding something against them from the onset. I wasn't going to begin my talks with a judgement against them already.

Imagine how this might apply to your world. Let's take a life negotiation for example. If the person you're about to talk with has wronged you in some way, done or said something that was hurtful to you, and you're about to enter into a *negotiation*[19] with them, how do you think holding what they'd done to you is going to work out for you both in your efforts to reach any reasonable agreement or resolution?

And how about a business negotiation when for one reason or another, the previous relationship just didn't work out? Walking into the negotiation room with a predetermined judgement of the person or company you're about to deal with will always be detrimental to your success. I'm not suggesting you walk in blindly. No. By now you've imagined every scenario, objection or white elephant in the prep phase and you're walking in with both eyes and ears wide open. You're choosing to approach it fresh, in order to create a new foundation on which you both can move forward on.

And what if an inside or outside source has told you something about the person/company you're going to be dealing with, and you hold *that* against them? Do you not think that this happens? It sadly does. Sometimes we have our own prejudices for no valid reason whatsoever. We should endeavor to leave all that behind if we're to reach agreements with others. We should be willing to give every person a chance to prove themselves worthy to us, as much as we prove ourselves to them.

---

[19] "Negotiation', as you now know, may be substituted for the word 'discussion'

Everybody deserves to be treated the way that we would like to be treated ourselves. We must be willing to separate the person from their previous actions (or what we've heard about them, should that be the case), while remaining professional and alert at all times if we're to reach the highest levels of success. Now I'm not saying 'don't be cautious.' Go in with both eyes and ears wide open but don't let the past keep you from building a new bridge. And, yeah, sometimes it just won't work out for whatever reason. Interestingly, sometimes one company simply isn't a fit with another. Or one person isn't a fit with another. At least you gave it a shot. And when the right 'fit' does come along, magic happens.

The Power Dynamic

Before you first meet with your negotiatee, especially in business, it's important to understand what is commonly referred to as the *power dynamic*. I briefly touched on this term earlier. Let me now explain what I mean.

In a hostage situation, for example, initially the hostage-taker has all the power. They have control of the hostages after all, so they get to 'call the shots' at first. My job was to bring them to a place where they would willingly relinquish that power and control to me - or at the very least, share it with me, so that we could work amicably together to resolve the conflict peacefully (i.e., find our solution), without injury or death to either hostage(s) or hostage-taker. I accomplished this "power shift" by being assertive, professional, invested and by asking questions focused on how we could work *together* to find the best solution. That, **and** by involving them in the process. If I couldn't establish value, trust or interest in what I proposed to them, I'd lose hostages.

Sometimes that was as simple as asking the hostage-taker, at the right moment through exploratory dialogue, what their greatest fear was. Not surprisingly, often the answer I got was, "I don't want to be shot if I come out." Asking the right question at the *right time*, rather than guessing, is crucial.

For you in your quest for an agreement or to get what you ask for, initially, it's your negotiatee who has all the power. In business, your negotiatee may be the one who holds the purse; who decides whether or not to trust you enough to give you their business. Regardless of what you're negotiating or asking from, your job will be to work at shifting that initial balance of power in your favor – placing you as an equal in their minds.

You accomplish this first through thorough preparation and later by discovering what it is they want and need, to be followed by the right proposal – in other words - using the **PIER™** as your guide. People agree with those they know, like and trust. And that's accomplished by asking first, soul listening next, using empathy and addressing their needs with what you have to offer to strategically demonstrate that your product or service is their best choice. Keep them feeling good about you and what you have to offer.

On doing the right thing

Nobody likes to be had. In business, for example, the buyers or investors want to feel secure that they're not only getting the right product or service for themselves or their company, but additionally, that they're investing in the right people behind the deal. Ones who deliver on their promises and solutions, not only in the moment, but over the long run as well. We want, expect and deserve reassurances that the person or persons we're entering into that relationship/deal with will deliver on their promises and provide us with the best customer service we're entitled to and expect, once the deal has been struck.

We tend to base most of our decisions from our gut (emotions) after all, so we hope the one we're dealing with is ethical and can be trusted. Our rational thinking comes later, after we've made the decision and the purchase or deal has been struck. Perhaps you can relate to a time you've had such an experience? You've just made a big purchase, and within 24 hours your rational thinking kicks in and is telling you that you made the wrong decision and dealt with the wrong person. Buyer's remorse sets in and you begin to analyze how the sale all went down. The salesperson *got* you. You were 'had' by an unethical salesperson and were manipulated in the hands of a professional self-serving idiot to the point where emotion overtook your rational thinking completely. I think most of us can relate to that. It doesn't only apply to the sales or business world either; it applies to life negotiations equally.

We've all bought into someone whose motives were unethical and self-serving. We've all been had. It's not a good feeling and has no place in any negotiation, no matter the circumstances. Remember guidepost number one: no manipulating?

Let's also remember that many negotiations are primarily emotion first. Successful negotiations require us to step away from the emotion and move towards rational thinking. We must understand that emotion will set in at some point, in us or our negotiatee, but it is our responsibility to move to solid rational decision-making to get the best for ourselves. It's a balancing act of strategic deployment.

Considerate control is important to success: it is never aggressive or demanding

If a person is in crisis, the odds are they feel like something important is missing - control. A person in crisis often feels like they have no control over their lives or circumstances, and that's also one of the significant stressors that pushes them into crisis in the first place. In negotiations, encouraging your negotiatee to be an active part of the decision-making process is vital to ultimately helping them out of (their) crisis and moving them forward along the PIER™ to an agreeable, safe and welcomed solution.

Encouraging your negotiatee to be part of the process starts by letting him/her talk while you express genuine interest and prod for more information, and it continues with your negotiatee taking an active part in the negotiation process.

One of the things I taught my officers at the police academy was that giving the other person a sense of control does not mean giving up *your* control. It's allowing them to be heard and understood first, then guiding them to a solution that benefits both of you next. 'Considerate' control is exactly that: maintaining control while considering the one you're negotiating with.

***

You don't have to be a bad ASS to be a badass.
***

Does a win-win approach to negotiations really work?

You may be wondering why I'm including a commentary on win-win negotiating. It's simply to caution you as you move forward in the negotiations and asking world. The way I see it, win-win is unfortunately very often a win-lose because it often invites unnecessary compromise. I'm not a fan. I've heard from many successful business negotiators that it simply doesn't work for them because somebody often ends up sacrificing too much, especially when dealing with a skilled or self-focused negotiator as their negotiatee.

In cases such as these, the skilled, cut-throat, butthead negotiator sitting across from you may suggest ridiculous offers, counting on you to meet somewhere in the middle – exactly where he/she wanted (and manipulated you) to be in the first place. If that's happened to you in one or more of your previous negotiations, it's time to readjust your thinking on the win-win mentality and dispense with 'win-win' as potentially fraudulent.

Personally, I never walk into a negotiation thinking win-win. I think mutually beneficial solutions and I always know what my bottom line is pre-negotiation. Negotiations are dynamic and flexible, so it makes sense to hear your negotiatee out, of course, but I encourage you to do so keeping your best interests in mind as you work on theirs to see if you can both reach an agreement you're both *happy* with, not one you feel or they feel has to be made. Is it give and take sometimes? Sure it is – but only within the boundary you're set to live with.

Think solutions within the margin of what you set in your prep phase, *pre*-negotiation. Never settle for less than what's right for you; and if you have in the back of your mind that this *needs* to be a win-win negotiation, you may be more likely to give more than what you were prepared to give. Doing so may lead to your financial demise, strained business relationships and unsatisfactory results. It may result in a win-lose for you. Know what your bottom line is before the negotiation begins. Be ready to say "No" if it gets to that stage. Be ready to walk.

If you're in a cut-throat, butthead negotiator's den, or if that arse has come to you, don't imagine for one moment that they have your best interests or genuine win-win in mind. They have *their* best interests in mind and solely *theirs,* and they're trained to manipulate. They're buttheads, after all.

If you feel pressured to make a decision that you know instinctively is wrong for you, it's time to slow things down. Never ignore your instinct. Pause for a few moments. Listen to your gut and *your* training. This may very well be a critical moment in the negotiations where tensions rise and emotion begs to take control. If up until that time you've approached your negotiation fairly and applied the principles of **PIER™**, then there is no cause to be embarrassed by slowing things down and using a lower, deeper, controlled voice to slow down the negotiation, taking immediate control and making your moves forward calculatively.

You accomplish this by asking a simple question. For example: "How do you expect me to accept that, John?" Your negotiatee may appear to get a little upset at your question; but remember that if it was his or her intention to lowball you, their rebuttal is *just an act*. It's an act meant to make you think win-win and have you fail and give in - and calculated to have them win by making you either feel like a bully or feel you're not playing fair. But remember that if you've been following PIER™, you ARE playing fair and have nothing to feel bad about. Ah, the levels a cutthroat will stoop to in order to bag their prize is shocking. Don't fall for it.

This applies to your life negotiations as much as it does to business – especially in a negotiation where emotions are running high. Slow it down. Don't feel pressured to agree to anything that does not work for you.

Despite whether it was just an act, you may encounter negotiations where someone does legitimately become upset. One of the most common reasons for this is that the other person may not feel that they have been heard, and frustration naturally surfaces. This can happen if you're not careful, or when you haven't deployed exploratory dialogue nearly enough to expose the heart of the matter. Think of some of your own personal relationships. Have you ever been with your significant other and been accused of not listening to them or providing them with the opportunity to do so without judgement?

With that in mind, this is a good time to define emotional intelligence.

A good negotiator learns how to harness another person's emotion as well as their own and use it to calm things down and get back on track by labeling the emotions that they've identified. Emotional intelligence generally involves three skills:

1. The ability to control your own emotions;

2. The ability to identify and control those of the negotiatee(s);

3. The ability to apply that intelligence to problem-solving.

If a negative emotion should arise in your negotiation, never ignore it.

Successful negotiations do require us to step away from the emotion when the time is right and move towards rational thinking to close successfully. As must your negotiatee. You must see emotion for what it is, understand that it's a big part of successful negotiating but move to solid rational decision-making to succeed. If you focus solely on a win-win approach, then you're leaving yourself open to being taken advantage of by ruthless and self-focused negotiators.

> Emotional intelligence generally involves three skills: the ability to control your own emotions; the ability to identify and control those of the negotiatee(s): and the ability to apply that intelligence to problem-solving.

Many smooth-talking professional negotiators will ask those with a win-win attitude to compromise while they have no intention of doing so themselves. Negotiate in good faith, yes, but be aware of the manipulators who tell you, "We need a little win-win here..." See that as a red flag. What are they asking you to give up? If you can't afford to give, don't. Be willing to walk away from the negotiation if it's not working for you, or propose something you can live with. Remember, when you give up too much, one default on that contract and they'll own you. Sometimes walking away makes you a bigger winner.

***

Sometimes your negotiatee just won't have
your best interests in mind, only theirs.
That's why it's so vital to remain focused on
the process and remain alert throughout.
Doing so provides you a greater chance to
get what you're after without giving
anything up you didn't count on giving up.

***

Not only must you be clear in/ your intent, you must look for the intent others have. Doing so keeps you on the alert and helps direct your negotiation.

Intent - Key Points

- Intention cannot be seen. It can only be felt and experienced through behavior. Intention is a representation of the motives and attitudes behind your actions.

- Be honest about your intent and should there be a time during your negotiation where you encounter hesitation or resistance, be prepared to vocalize what your intent is, again.

- Never ignore nonverbal messages or cues that you become aware of in the negotiation. Identify them, call them out *softly* for what they appear to be and take the necessary steps to address them completely before moving forward.

- Many negotiators focus on the end first. That's something you can't control. Focus on the means rather. By doing that, you'll have a greater chance of an excellent outcome.

- Just because another negotiator has had a failed negotiation does not mean that a secondary negotiator can't succeed.

- Negotiate the way would like to be negotiated with.

- Be grateful for even those negotiations and life experiences that don't work out for you, providing you've learned from them.

- If you do make a mistake, it's not the end of the world. Some negotiators and business people believe that if they blew it the first time, the game's over. Not necessarily. It depends on the circumstances.

- Understand that in most negotiations (this includes sales and even in dating), the person you are entering the negotiation with often has all the power. They may either have the money or the right to put a stop to the 'negotiation' before you even ask your question. Your focus will be on providing reasons of value and trust to first have them listen, then take them through the PIER™ to a 'yes.'

- Never behave unethically. Doing so will have its consequences and your chances of ever dealing with the person you've manipulated will be destroyed, as will your reputation. Always do the right thing.

- Win-win doesn't always mean everybody wins. Be cautious of those who propose win-win.

- Not only must you be aware of your intent, but you must also look at the intent of the one you're negotiating with as well. Doing so helps you remain sharp and arms you with an awareness that helps you to not be taken advantage of.

Call to action:

- Before entering into your very next negotiation, be it in life or in business, take a few moments. Stop. First, ask yourself what your intent is (what you plan to achieve and how you plan to achieve it). Follow this by promising yourself that you will not only convey your intent (in part or in full) to the one you'll be negotiating with but that you will follow through in your actions and behavior. Be willing to say what you mean and show it in everything you do from that point on. Make your words matter.

Chapter Five

————·⦁◆⦁·————

PRINCIPLE NUMBER 3: ENTRANCE & ENGAGEMENT

> "People will forget what you said. People
> will forget what you did. But people will
> never forget how you made them feel."
> **Maya Angelou**

The 'E' in PIER™ Negotiating: (Entrance &) Engagement

The above quote has been one of my favorites for as far back as I can remember. It only seems fitting to begin this chapter with a memorable quote that exemplifies what this chapter is about to examine.

I don't know about you, but I've experienced this several times. Whether it was a keynote talk that I delivered, a performance I'd given, or a work-related encounter, I've met people I'd connected with several months or years earlier who felt an instant, warm connection to me. It wasn't necessarily what they remembered I'd said, but as the above quote makes very clear, I believe it was the way I'd made them feel that made the difference.

We can never underestimate the power of making a memorable and positive first impression. As they say, "you never get a second chance to make a good first impression."

After being selected as a successful candidate for my mission to Jordan in 2004, I was put through a battery of tests to determine my physical and mental state before deployment. Naturally, the United Nations and the Canadian government, for that fact, don't want to be sending a peacekeeper on a mission they are unfit for. Concerns of returning with posttraumatic stress disorder is high on that list and I was sent to a psychiatrist whose job it was to determine my mental qualifications.

After filling out a 500-question psychological evaluation test, I met with the psychiatrist to discuss the results. He also wanted to question me about my personal past. I got the feeling from the moment I walked in to see him that he was disinterested in conducting the evaluation. Nevertheless, we got through it, but not without a few bumps along the way. He felt I had a problem with authority, but I assured him that I did not have a problem with authority, I had a problem with incompetent, *stupid* authority. The 500-question evaluation had apparently highlighted what he perceived to be a character flaw in me and a potential reason to prevent my deployment.

My wife at the time was next to be interviewed. In her conversation with the doctor, she happened to mention that my father had killed himself when I was 17. Well, that didn't go over well at all with him and he promptly called me back in for a second interview.

He expressed concerns about my deployment, citing posttraumatic stress on my return as a high probability. He based that on my father's suicide and what it 'must have done' to me. At this stage of our engagement, a strong 'objection' had slipped in. It was my job to address that objection and provide sound reasons why the objection was unfounded, if I was to succeed.

To counter the objection, I reminded the doctor that he had my complete file at his disposal and that I'd been on the police service for over twenty years. I also reminded him that I was a competent hostage negotiator, peer counsellor and that I had been a supervisor of over thirty officers for a number of years. I additionally invited him to examine my service record, which included working on homicides and other serious sexual crimes in the capacity of a detective and a number of commendations.

I ended with: "Doctor, would you not agree that if I was imbalanced and unfit for this mission, in any way, evidence of that would have already surfaced somewhere in my career? (Pause) I assure that that I am mentally fit for this mission. I understand that the decision is yours to make, doctor, but preventing me from being deployed would be a serious mistake."

The idiot signed off on my deployment, but he didn't seem happy about it. When I think back on it, it *was* a negotiation, and one I was prepared to handle despite whatever objection arose in the engagement phase, which is what you must do as well. His obvious disinterest in the process made it difficult to reach an amicable agreement, but not impossible. I'd dressed professionally for the interview, greeted him with a warm smile, firm handshake and conducted myself as a competent professional throughout. But I noticed that he was not maintaining eye contact and that he appeared uninterested from the onset. Despite this, I knew I had to forge ahead, even though the guy was a complete butthead.

***

Sometimes you'll have to negotiate with buttheads. Keep calm, remain professional and forge ahead. Even buttheads can be negotiated with.

***

When I stop to imagine what you might encounter in your life and business negotiations, it's no different. We negotiate in real life circumstances and at times the stakes are extremely high. How prepared you are and how you conduct yourself throughout the negotiation (your engagement) will make a significant difference in the outcome. Had I not pointed out the **value** I had to offer the mission (hostage negotiator, peer counselor, supervisor and accomplished investigator) or countered the objection that arose, I never would have made it to Jordan.

I didn't like that man and nor do I to this day. It's how he made me feel that I recall the most. Enough on that. Let's move on, but you get the idea.

The previous chapter on Intent made it clear that intentions are not something that can be seen unless they are directly connected to behaviors that reflect the value of the original intent. The two must work together and act as your Ying and Yang, so to speak, of negotiation. Intentions are represented by accompanying actions and guidepost number four appeals to us to demonstrate our intent through meaningful and thoughtful behaviors as well as action. We must be clear about our intention and that relates directly to the first principle of PIER™ – in our preparation phase.

Not only must we have our intention solidified in our minds and hearts, we must also seek to discover the intent of the one we'll be negotiating with. It helps to tell the person we're negotiating with what our intention is and it helps us if they reciprocate in kind by informing us what theirs is. When this does not happen, it's our right and responsibility to ask what their intent is – and watch for any signs of uncertainty or deception.

Never shall we stoop to a state of neediness no matter the circumstances or negotiation we find ourselves in. Begging and pleading have no place in any negotiation, be it in life or in business. We now understand that mistakes are not the end of the world and not necessarily the end of the negotiation. We must always deploy our best intentions, and by doing so, our overall state will convey truth, confidence and purpose to the one we're with. And how do you accomplish that, exactly?

Make your entrance memorably positive

A good entrance is a great entrance. Never underestimate the power of making your best *entrance* possible. First impressions are lasting impressions.

Up until now, we've examined the importance of preparation and intent. Now it's time to meet your negotiatee. Maybe you already know this person, and now it's time to move forward with the negotiation and ask for something you'd like. Remember how I suggested you prepare for your negotiation as you would for your first date? It's now time to turn on that charisma and deploy your PIER™ savvy, baby!

New research tells us that it only takes 1/10th of a second to make a first impression[20]. Good or bad. Knowing this will help you

---

[20] APS – Association of Psychological Science:
http://www.psychologicalscience.org/index.php/publications/observer/2006/july-06/how-many-seconds-to-a-first-impression.html

cement the concept that you're being evaluated the instant you meet your negotiatee. Understanding this concept will help you get into the right frame of mind before you ever approach your negotiation. As much as you will be unconsciously (or consciously) assessing the other person's body language, appearance and approachability to determine if you can like, know and trust that individual, he/she will likewise be doing the same to you.

The first few seconds you meet someone will be your most important ones, and they may also be forming an opinion of you in that 1/10th of a second. Make the wrong first impression in that instant, and you may have difficulty recovering from it. This involves dressing correctly for the occasion, having your best smile on display, being aware of what your body language is transmitting to your negotiatee and making sure that your handshake is professional, firm and welcoming. You're being evaluated from the moment you first meet.

Let's face it, we all make assessments of one another in the first milliseconds we meet, don't we? That's a good thing. Our primitive brains have programmed us to survive, and with that in mind, it scrambles through scenario after scenario deciphering a number of things, depending on the circumstances: "Is this someone I can trust? Do they mean me harm? Are they friend or foe? Are they trustworthy? Do they have status and authority over me? Are they competent, reliable and likable? Are they a potential partner?" You get the idea – no matter what the setting, meeting new people triggers survival instincts within us, and we make choices based on what our sixth-sense (our guts) tell us. It's no different when we meet someone to do business with or go on a first date.

All this takes place in the matter of those first milliseconds. We are hard-wired by our prehistoric primitive brains to consider these unknowns, and we must consider these evaluations because our very survival or good/bad fortune depends on it. We instinctively conclude whether it's safe to engage any further with the other individual or individuals. Whether it's getting on that elevator with strangers or walking that darkened street, our instinctive reactions play a serious role in our decisions. That 'sixth-sense' kicks in and in a matter of milliseconds a decision is reached.

When meeting someone for the first time, as in a business setting, for example, we begin with a simple, genuine and friendly introduction. How you introduce yourself to the person you've just met or who is sitting across from you and how you describe what your goals, motivations and intentions are will help the negotiation process get off on the right foot.

Dropping titles, whenever possible, and behaving as an equal in the negotiation setting will level the playing field. Showing respect and building rapport are among the very best strategies for persuading others. Hostage negotiators know this principle extremely well; one of our first objectives is to slow the process down and build a relationship with the hostage taker. Once a sense of human connection and understanding develops, hostage negotiators find that we have a much better chance of resolving the crisis successfully. Spend time discussing personal or interesting non-negotiation related matters at the beginning of your meeting and occasionally return to them (more on this in the conversation and discussion section to follow). A cordial greeting is a good place to start, followed by a simple conversation opener.

Secondly, to foster later collaboration, try to set a constructive, positive tone; greet the other person warmly and try to signal early on that you hope the two of you will be able to collaborate well together. In business negotiations, try one of the following approaches early on in the negotiation: Once you've warmed up to them and them to you in the conversation/rapport building phase, make the transition from conversation to discussion: "Let me start by getting your perspective on this. What's important for me to know and to understand?" or "Let me listen to you first. Help me understand what you're looking to get".

I cannot emphasize enough the importance of beginning your interactions/negotiations by taking time to build trust and rapport and setting a positive tone for the negotiation. For most negotiations to be successful, you must be prepared to invest **time** into it. Instead of talking about your wants early on, ask specific questions and listen for insights about the other person's interests. For example, in business negotiations, you might say, "Let me first begin by understanding your concerns/wants here."

Depending on the other parties' willingness to share information, you may choose to share some information about your own interests with your negotiatee if that gets the conversation going. It's not necessary or wise to reveal everything just yet, but by sharing some of your interests, you invite the other to do the same and that leads to creative problem-solving dialogue later on.

In hostage negotiations, one of the things we strived for was for the hostage taker or person in crisis to vent and to tell us what their concerns were – their perspective, or POV (point of view). Hostage takers and distressed individuals have a million things running through their heads. Our role was to help them express those concerns and later help them focus on mutual interests and solutions. We begin with the end in sight, sure, but not as our primary focus. Once we identified with their concerns, we invited a discussion about creative options.

This type of negotiation is called an *interest-based negotiation*, and is that not what we should also be doing in our life negotiations as well – listening to the others point of view first, ahead of our own? Sometimes it's extremely hard being in a relationship when something goes wrong. Many of us tend to react to the moment instead of assessing it and proceeding with caution for clarity and resolution. This knee-jerk reaction has no place in any relationship, be it business or personal. Here is the ideal time to 'listen with the soul' and ask questions. Talking comes later. If we get loud and react in anger, no one gets anywhere. We yell louder, and they listen less – or it triggers something worse. Use this in a hostage negotiation and see what happens.

Your very first impression in business negotiations, for example, is no different, and the outcome of your interaction will greatly depend on what kind of first impression you make. First impressions are more heavily based on body language – the non-verbal cues we send out, willingly or unwillingly; major decisions can be reached in the first few moments you meet someone. Right or wrong, we base our reasons to engage or disengage in the first few seconds of meeting someone.

Knowing this is one of the advantage points I mentioned earlier. Knowing yourself and consciously making a good first impression is imperative. Think before you walk in for that first meeting or any meeting for that matter. Focus on your posture, your smile, how you're dressed for the meeting and how you will greet your negotiatee.

This may sound very simple, but it is a necessary step in making a good first impression. How's your handshake? People evaluate handshakes consciously and unconsciously depending on the person that you're dealing with. Imagine shaking hands with someone whose grip is limp, or whose hands are sweaty. Entire courses are taught on how to shake a hand correctly. Watch any video of politicians who are in a position of power and authority to see how they shake hands. Greater success is often found in the details.

These small details are anything but "small details". You have but a few milliseconds to make a good first impression and believe me, if your first impression is a bad one, you may never recover from it. The person across from you, the person you're meeting for the first time is assessing you as much as much as you're assessing him/her. Remember, we are all similar.

Imagine yourself meeting someone for the first time. What are you basing your judgement on? Your reptilian brain is assessing the interaction to determine whether or not you can trust the person that you're meeting. It's no different for them. Check yourself out thoroughly first. Would *you* want and like to meet *you*?

What I can tell you is that in my world, that first few seconds of any negotiation or interrogation/contact was crucial to my overall success because not only was I was dealing with life and death or a potential confession, I wanted to succeed and make a lasting connection. You never know when you'll meet that person again and under what circumstances. I knew that the first few seconds were critical to establishing the right tone. That's why your entrance and your engagement is so vitally important to your overall success in any of life and business negotiation. Make them count. Let me provide you with a story to illustrate this point.

How using the PIER™ Negotiating principles worked on a sexual offender

During my stint as a sexual assault investigator, I was handed an investigation involving the savage rape of several young boys by a teenaged male babysitter. In one horrific case, a 9-year-old male victim was almost strangled to death. It was clear that I was dealing with a power aggressive serial rapist who could easily kill one of his next victims if he wasn't apprehended. There were half a dozen reports, and the level of violence was escalating in each case. The case was initially an 'unsub.'[21] All I had was a description, the 'possibility' the young rapist (believed to be 14 – 16 years old) lived in the same low-income housing projects as his victims, and a first name: I'll call him 'Aaron.'

Why so little information, you ask? Unfortunately, the single parents who lived in that complex who hired him as their babysitter didn't do their due diligence in researching who they were hiring to babysit their precious children. Aaron simply answered ads he found in the lobby of buildings looking for babysitters. And midway through his raping spree, he changed locations: three ghastly sexual assaults in one complex and three in another, miles away.

I was able to get an artist's sketch made of what he looked like from my collective witnesses which later helped me immensely in identifying him. I pounded the pavement for days in search of someone who might recognize the sketch or him by name. That footwork paid off. I got a full name and an address. Once I positively identified him (after much surveillance and that groundwork), I made an early morning arrest and took him into custody. The interrogation - or rather, the *negotiation* was next. Once I had him in the interrogation room and informed him of the grounds for the arrest, I dropped the purpose and facts of the case and began to establish rapport[22]. That involved dropping my title of 'detective' and asking him to call me by my first name. Remember, whenever

---

[21] Unsub: Unidentified Subject
[22] See 'Moving from entrance to engagement to conversation to discussion' following next

possible, you must do the same. Drop their title and yours whenever you can. Invite your negotiatee to call you by your first name.

Aaron had been thoroughly apprised of his right to counsel, and as a young offender, there were many additional legal steps I followed pre-interrogation to ensure that he understood the level of jeopardy he was facing before I could ever proceed with any interrogation. Once I was satisfied that he understood his extensive rights, I began the negotiation with a simple conversation to get to know him. Doing so in any negotiation is a key to rapport building. I separated the person from the deeds he had committed. I found some common ground between us, and we talked about nothing specific. I watched and evaluated his body language to establish what is called homeostasis (his norm when not under stress) and assessed the best time to move from simple conversation to 'discussion' – the meat of the interrogation.

That didn't take long, and at the end of our time together, Aaron had confessed to all six sexual assaults – and he *thanked* me. I had connected with him, and a relationship was built. Did that mean I accepted his behavior as a rapist? Not at all, and he knew it. He got so comfortable with me that I gave him hell for what he had done and he was ok with that. A bond had been made. Perhaps I was the only one in a long time to treat him with dignity and respect, and that's why he felt the bond. It often happens that way.

So many criminals have told me that I was the first one to treat them decently in a long time, or ever – not even their families had. This I'm certain accounted for much of my success as an interrogator. Now, imagine your approach using my methods in your life and business negotiations. Maybe you'll be the first one in a long time to treat your negotiatee in this way, and why wouldn't they want to give you what you ask for using that approach? Now, back to Aaron.

The story doesn't end there. Aaron was detained in custody and later confessed in court to all of the sexual assaults I had arrested him for. He was convicted and sentenced to just under two years in a juvenile detention center – not nearly enough for the horrendous crimes he had committed and the danger to society I knew him to be. But as a young offender, the court treated him as such. Aaron had come to like and respect me in that very short period of time we spent together, and I attribute that to entrance and engagement, not to mention preparation, intent and relationship building: PIER™. I was not in a hurry to get to the meat of why I had arrested him. I wanted to know the person first.

By using PIER™ Negotiating, he cooperated even though by doing so and confessing meant he was going to fry for his crimes. Okay, not fry. As a young offender, he merely got seared. Moving along, partway into his sentence, another detective received case files involving Aaron as a suspect. They were previously unsolved cases (unsubs) because no name had been attached to the description, but now that I had identified Aaron, all this information was entered into a violent offender's classification program, easily accessible to all law enforcement officers across the country, and out popped Aaron as a suspect.

The detective assigned the Aaron files was Rick, also an SAU (Sexual Assault Unit) detective and he drove to the juvenile detention center where Aaron was being held and took a shot at clearing the cases by trying to secure confessions from Aaron. He returned to the office and informed me that he got nowhere with Aaron, but that Aaron had sent me a "hello" he wanted to make sure I got. I offered to take over Rick's case files and drive up to interview Aaron myself.

Rick gladly handed the files to me, and the next day I took a trip to see Aaron at the juvenile detention center he was being detained in, a distance outside our jurisdiction. Aaron was happy to see me; and after going through all the legal cautions and warnings he was all too familiar with, I simply asked Aaron if he had committed the offenses for which he was suspected. One by one we went through them. In each case, Aaron didn't hesitate a second to nod his head 'yes,' admitting his crimes with a sheepish yes and 'sorry I didn't tell you, Paul' to boot. It was that easy. He provided me with details and full confessions. And he did so almost happily. It was as though he was chatting with a good friend and was relieved to get it off his chest. Surprising somewhat to me, I'll admit – only because I believed Aaron to be a true psychopath. But that's another story. And *this* is an example of the power of building rapport and beginning with conversations first.

My negotiation communications model: Moving from entrance to engagement, to conversation to discussion. *The discussion *is* the negotiation

As for me, without exploratory dialogue and simple conversation first in my interrogations and many other negotiations I've entered into, the person I was speaking with would never open up enough to let me in. This rarely was the case with my hostage negotiations, however. In hostage negotiations, as in some business and life negotiations, you do have to get right down to it. It's just the way it is sometimes.

Imagine for a moment a detective entering an interrogation room to interrogate a suspect accused of a serious crime. Would that suspect be welcoming the detective with open arms, ready to confess everything without a second thought, simply because they were asked, as Aaron had with me after we had bonded? Nope. That suspect wouldn't happily be open to answering any questions about the crime under investigation without the right approach first being used. His/her thoughts would be focused on his/her own fears, best interests, survival and the distrust he/she feel for me. I wouldn't matter squat to them. This is where so many agreement seekers mess up.

Suspects under interrogation, in general, wouldn't welcome a thing I was saying and would get their backs up only to deny everything as strongly as they could – or simply remain silent, invoking their right to do so, without the right approach first being used. They care too much about freedom, survival, and costs, and would be in fight or flight mode.

Now imagine yourself in a negotiation of your own where the stakes are high, and rapport has not yet been established - is your negotiatee not experiencing this mistrust and hesitation themselves? I suggest to you that they are. If they don't know you, they have no reason to trust you or like you, just yet. You must give them a reason to. They're not anxious to part with their money without seeing value in doing so first - if that's what you're after, especially if they feel that you may be there to take advantage of them. They're evaluating you as much as you're evaluating them.

To summarize the foregoing then, focus first on making a connection and building rapport. It doesn't have to take long. I never lost sight of what I was there to do (my intent) and I focused on the moment, the process and the journey first and foremost, and not solely on the outcome. Prepare to do the same. Imagine your approach and conversation before you meet. Have an idea in mind but not a script. Be flexible and dynamic.

Had I focused on the outcome first, I would have jeopardized my success, as you will yours. Doing so is not 'interests based' negotiations because it does not involve the negotiatee. By focusing on rapport-building and trust first, I knew when the right time was to move it to the next stage – to the 'discussion' (which is the negotiation as you'll soon see). In the interrogation/negotiation with a suspect for example, once trust and rapport had been established, I moved toward my intended objective – looking for the truth.

That approach worked so well that most guilty suspects were by then relaxed and open. Their body language went from being defensive to being visibly relaxed; and they confessed when they found value in what I offered, many thanking me on their way out of the interrogation room even though they knew that by having confessed, they would be facing a prison sentence. And it didn't stop there. When I encountered them in court on their trial date, most would wave at me, smile and call me by my first name - something the defense lawyers absolutely hated. Some of them would then plead guilty after simply seeing me in court.

Why, you may ask? Because I'd provided them with a solution that helped them save face; I had met their emotional needs by having established a human connection and bond with them. I made them feel good about the deal. They got to know me, like me and trust me. They saw value in confessing, and they didn't want to be on opposing sides of the courtroom from me I suppose.

What I know for certain is that it works. Besides, the 'deal' had by then been signed – the confession had been recorded. Did that always work? No, not always, but in most cases it did; and that was good enough for me and for the prosecution obviously, not to mention the many witnesses that would be spared having to testify. Yes, some of *your* negotiatees will deal with you not only because you have a good solution to offer, but because of the bond and relationship you establish with them. That's how powerful rapport-building is. And it works equally well in life and in business as it does in hostage negotiations and interrogations. It's not always about who has the strongest bargaining power. It's about how we can work together in satisfying the humanity in our varying needs.

Conversation, then Discussion – the two-step Negotiation and Asking order

There is a general order of communication to successful negotiations. I say general because we know opening with a proposal is sometimes called for, but for negotiations we plan for, a simple order on how the negotiation should unfold is recommended. This order has been proven to work – not only in negotiations but when dealing with conflict and other important matters.

Negotiations must involve both conversation *and* discussion, as much as they must involve active/soul listening *and* asking the right questions, which I'll get to more in depth as you read on. Negotiating and asking involves communicating with and without *purpose*. You may be trying to wrap your mind around that last line but hang on for a moment, I'll explain.

It's important to understand the difference between conversation and discussion before you meet your negotiatee because you'll need each, in that order whenever possible, to reach a solid and meaningful agreement using the principles of hostage negotiation (and PIER™) when you later meet with him/her. This is not difficult to grasp. Remember how I told you that I intend to keep things simple? Here I'll endeavor to do just that. Let me explain what I mean.

Conversation, as I see it, is an exchange between two or more people that helps establish rapport and connection. It's non-specific chit-chat with no precise goal (purpose) in mind other than to enjoy each other's company, get to know each other, get comfortable with each other and often to simply have fun and pass the time. Watch children playing in the park. That's conversation. That's having fun. That's bonding.

A *discussion*, on the other hand, **has** a specific goal and purpose in mind. It is 'with specific purpose,' whereas conversation, although having value, is non-specific (the 'without' purpose, so to speak.)

As you make your way through the rest of this book, you'll understand why it's important to start with conversation first – chatting to get to know a bit about each other and build a bond - *whenever* possible and when time and circumstances permit. You've already read a few of my stories that have demonstrably demonstrated the importance of connection and rapport building through conversation.

Conversation first establishes that all-important connection (the rapport), that which is vitally important as the foundation on which to move ahead to asking the right, and sometimes tough questions, for the purpose of eliciting the vital information you need. It provides you an open window into the thoughts, concerns and motivations of the person you're negotiating with – a step that takes you closer to actual resolution and solution, and one that helps build a connection of trust and likeability.

A conversation is a simple, non-specific chat. It can lead nowhere in particular – just a simple exchange of thoughts and ideas to pass the time and enjoy the moment and the person you're with: it helps to establish a friendly rapport, and it can take you places you'd never have imagined.

A simple conversation can also lead to a life-long connection. It's a bus stop encounter, a friendly coffee shop chat with a friend or stranger, a first date "getting to know each other" exploratory exchange or the sounds of children playing together having the times of their lives. It's often intended to draw people closer together – to establish a human connection which we all need so desperately. It can be the cement that binds two or more people together; the glue that creates the sweet moments in life; or, if misdirected, misused or abused, a wedge that separates us.

***

Starting your 'ask' or negotiation with small talk to build rapport needn't be a long, dragged out affair, but doing so will vastly improve your chances of getting what you're after.

***

Whenever possible, begin each planned negotiation with a conversation

Whenever I interrogated a suspect, I would never begin with the *interrogation*[23] (the discussion) first. I've mentioned this more than once – it's that important. I was in no hurry to get to that phase prematurely – to the "confession," that is, as some call it. I had come to realize the importance of establishing rapport through exploratory and simple conversation first in my gradual search for the truth. I knew the importance of building that much-needed rapport; and I knew that doing so begins with a simple conversation; sharing your humanness, so to speak. I understood the importance of sitting across from my suspect and putting him/her at ease, tearing down their walls of defense, doubt and distrust first and building bridges and human connection in their place. I separated the person from the crime, setting the crime aside at first while I focused on the person. Neglecting that vital step meant jeopardizing my results and what I was after - the truth.

---

[23] I suppose this is as good a time as any to address the police 'interrogation.' Nobody likes that word. We'd prefer to hear the word 'interview.' I'll be changing it shortly to soften it up

I wanted each suspect to get to know me a bit (nothing I wouldn't *want* to disclose – this is not an intimate relationship after all) as I got to know him/her first. I wanted them to see me as an understanding, non-judgmental human being and not only as a cop; as someone that they would feel comfortable enough to tell me what I wanted to know. I accomplished this by first inviting them to talk about themselves and not about the crime they were suspected of having committed.

"Conversation first" is a valuable first step to overall negotiation success. It allows for a free-flowing exchange, and it sets the mood. Although the purpose of the interrogation had been initially outlined, (the intent or purpose of our meeting: i.e., "Ben, I'm investigating the murder of John Doe and you've been named a suspect. Before we talk about that, I want to take a few moments to find out more about you – who I'm dealing with, who you are - without relying on what others have told me.")

The objective of the interrogation was not re-visited until after I had established a connection of trust and rapport had been established with the individual under investigation. This doesn't have to take long. A few minutes is all it takes in many cases. Sometimes it does take longer depending on the seriousness of what's at stake. You'll know when to take more time.

As for my approach to establishing this bond, I'd look for things we had in common to chat about, and I would make sure to make them feel important and equal – not as prey for me to hunt, capture, manipulate or lock up. A warm smile, professional handshake and demonstrating a genuine interest in them went a long way.

One of the ways I would go about accomplishing this was by telling the suspect right from the beginning that I was not there to judge them or to find them guilty of anything. Because I wasn't. I would tell them that I was only after the truth. I wanted to make the suspect sitting across from me feel ok having me in the room. I wanted to establish a relationship with them because most people will deal with you only *after* they know you, like you and trust you - and what better way of getting that to happen than to strike up a casual conversation on your way to building strong rapport? With that in mind, imagine what kind of a conversation you could enter into with one of your negotiatees or someone of interest to you.

From conversation to the discussion: The discussion *is* the negotiation

I want you now to substitute the word *interrogation* with the word *discussion*. The discussion is the negotiation as earlier noted. This should not be hard to understand because as earlier noted, conversation is rapport building: non-specific chatter. There are two simple blocks to a negotiation model: block "A" is conversation. It obviously and should come before block "B" – discussion. *Interrogation, discussion,* and the actual *negotiation* all involve specifics – specific and direct questions, specific goals and specific outcomes. Understand this pre-negotiation must: the discussion *is* the negotiation. Having vocalized the purpose of the negotiation, engaged in non-specific conversation, and built rapport, we now transition into to discussing their wants as well as our own.

Remember, a discussion is simply a two-way exchange between two or more people with a **specific** goal or purpose, as distinct from the type of casual conversation described earlier in this chapter. It is, indeed, the negotiation. Unlike a *casual* conversation, a 'discussion,' within the context of negotiation, has a clearly-defined/specific purpose: what we're after. Now is the time to work toward agreements. Should you encounter an unexpected opportunity that calls to lead with a proposal, seize it and start with block "B" (the discussion) but don't overlook using block "A" to finish it off. It builds rapport.

How to plan your Questions

So, what exactly do we say or ask in a negotiation to reach our intended agreement? Everybody needs answers to their questions or their problems, but just as importantly, people need to picture what they'll be getting from you in return. They need a vision and to establish value in the exchange for themselves, and so, you must create it for them. Questions and discussions are excellent ways to create that vision and will serve to help them visualize and imagine outcome and also to reach a decision.

Whenever possible, you want to keep the negotiation in the world of your negotiatee, creating valuable images that lead to decisions on their part. By asking the right kinds of questions and by directing the discussion, it allows us to get more of an insight into the other person's world so that we can uncover what concerns, objections or visions they have that we should address. This helps us move them forward in making a decision that involves saying 'yes' to you. And this is where I'll stress the importance of asking the right kinds of questions.

Questions, after all, lead to answers. And answers are one thing we're after in our negotiations, aren't they? As a professional interrogator, I ask very direct, close-ended questions - at first. Quite simply, they were verb led questions requiring a simple "yes" or "no" answer. For example, in the case of a homicide, my question may have simply been, "Sam, did you kill Mary Smith?" And there are only two legitimate answers to that question: "Yes" or "No." For an interrogator who is after a yes or no answer and a clue in how they answer that direct question, that's fine. Following whatever answer they provided me, it led to more inquiry on my part. But *you're* not after a confession to a murder now, are you? So not only do you have to use the science of asking the right questions, you also have to use the *art* of asking the right questions.

Questions that begin with a verb such as "Can," "Will," "Do" and "Is" for example will simply elicit one of three responses: "Yes," "No," or "Maybe." That's not what you're after in *your* negotiation. Remember, you want to create a positive vision and get more information from your negotiatee. So, asking a question like, "Can you do this?" will provide you with little information to help lead your negotiatee to a decision. Not only that, it may also make the person sitting across from you feel uneasy, as though you were asking them to do too much or leading them too quickly to make a decision. By asking verb led questions, it may create a sense of anxiousness in your negotiatee, and that's not what you want to do in any negotiation. Don't propose a question that seems to the negotiatee to be taking away their right to say "No."

As a former cop, one of the questions I would often ask to encourage cooperation or to elicit more information was quite simple: "Is there anything I can say or do that would have you reconsider..." Notice how this kind of question might encourage more than a yes or no response. Now you may be thinking, "Well that question could easily be answered with a simple 'yes' or 'no.' And indeed it can.

More often than not, in a negotiation that you have been working at with your negotiatee for some time, if you've established rapport and never made them feel "un-okay," then you're likely to enter their world when they honestly answer you whether there is something or not. And what if they were to simply respond with a one-word answer "No"? Simply repeat their answer as though it were a question, "No"?... Remember that technique? But that scenario is not likely to happen.

What you want to do in a negotiation is to ask *discussion-led* questions. Questions that beg to be answered by more than just one word: open-ended question. Choosing how you frame your questions is extremely important in any kind of negotiation or effective communication. And we're dealing with both here.

Consider the differences between these questions for example:

"Is this the biggest issue/stumbling block that you see xxx?" As opposed to, "What is the biggest issue/stumbling block you see here?"

Or, "Is this price I'm offering our services for too expensive for you?" as opposed to, "What price do you see yourself comfortably paying for the services I'm offering you here?"

Or, "Is this proposal I'm offering here complete enough for you?" as opposed to, "How can I make my proposal to you more complete and attractive for you?"

Do you see the differences? The second set of questions empowers your negotiatee, providing them with a sense of control to a degree but more importantly, it provides them with the message that you're not there to push them into making the wrong decision. It gives them the sense that you're working with them, and after it's all said and done, in any kind of negotiation, is that not exactly what we're after?

Asking open-ended discussion led questions will help your negotiatee feel comfortable enough to open the dialogue of communication and express what it is that they want or need, which in turn will help you immensely. Once all the information is out, that will help both of you reach a solid, well thought out logic-based decision. One you can both live with. Remember that the way in which you frame your questions will be a reflection of you and will also help you to get more information allowing you to plant a seed in your negotiatee's mind. For example, in business, if you have a product that your negotiatee wants, instead of simply asking, "Can you get by without this awesome product?" consider asking, "How can you get by without this awesome product?" You can hear the difference.

The first question "Can you get by without this awesome product?" is going to give you a one-word answer, whereas the second question, "How can you get by without our awesome product?" encourages more thought in the negotiatee and consequently, will lead to more dialogue between the two of you. Keep it light and playful but on point. Can you see the subtle yet important differences in taking time to create the best questions? The second offering of well-framed questions prompts the negotiatee to consider whether or not they can get by without it, and also serves to help them verbalize their thoughts. Now this applies to your life negotiations just as much. Consider who you'll be negotiating with and what questions will give you the most information to use.

Keep your questions simple. You're not in a courtroom, after all. Ask one question at a time, unlike a defense attorney in a courtroom of law who will ask several questions at once. Defense lawyers do this for a reason. By doing so, it confuses the witness, and the witness is likely to give the wrong answer because they have become confused. You certainly don't want to confuse your negotiatee, nor do you want to make them feel anxious.

One of the things to consider as being extremely important is what your body language is saying to your negotiatee as you negotiate and ask the questions. Are your words consistent with your body language? Is your tone of voice a soft, non-threatening tone? Are you excitedly asking your questions, or do you have a non-threatening late-night radio hosts' kind of voice? Are you leaning in too quickly or aggressively or clasping your hands in anticipation as you ask a question? Or are you in control of your body and aware of what your body is transmitting?

I've mentioned that I've been witness to many interrogations being conducted by inexperienced detectives and constables that I just shook my head in disbelief to. They wanted answers and cooperation, but the way in which they went about getting it was harsh, sharp, anxious and aggressive. They towered over the suspect in a demanding, unrelenting way, most often accusatory from the get-go. And if they sat across from him/her, they would often move in for the confession (the agreement) far too quickly and far too aggressively. This did nothing to help their interrogation along. In fact, it closed the suspect up to being open and willing to disclose and cooperate.

Being friendly and playful helps: but choose when, with whom, and how much

When I was on mission in the Middle East, I had the opportunity to visit the Souk in Amman - an outdoor marketplace where merchants had honed their interpersonal communication and negotiation skills so well that they could draw people into their tents and start negotiating and haggling over prices effortlessly and immediately. They do this so incredibly well that it occurred to me at the time that in the hands of a skilled merchant, I had to be careful! I had to approach each encounter in a very playful way, otherwise, I could easily be hooked. And so I did. They would make an offer, and I would make a counter- offer, no matter how ridiculously low it sounded. But the playfulness never left my voice and never left theirs either. Using that approach helped me get a few deals I otherwise would have walked away from or paid much more to get. We met somewhere we could both live with.

When people are in the right frame of mind, they are more willing to collaborate and to problem-solve. The right attitude, tone of voice and humanness helps you get there. The important thing to remember is to try to keep the negotiation playful and relaxed whenever possible. Now I understand that when you're in a serious negotiation you're not likely to keep it 'playful,' nor should you. In the case of a hostage negotiation, I would never bring out the playful approach, but I would always try to keep it relaxed. Choose when, with whom, and how much.

Body language: yours

I've discussed body language throughout this book because it's so vitally important to your overall success as a negotiator and agreement seeker. I cannot overemphasize this. Having the right body language is so vitally important to your success. I promised you more on body language in the last chapter, and here it comes!

After returning from my peacekeeping mission in 2006, I was sent for extensive training at the Canadian Police College in Ottawa, Ontario to become a polygraph examiner. A large segment of this training was devoted to lie detecting and body language – from listening to the very words uttered by the person across from me, to actively watching every move in their body, face and eyes to gauge whether or not they were being truthful or deceptive, open or closed. I had studied this in my earlier Detective years, but this extensive polygraph training brought it to a whole new level.

What I discovered was never to ignore what a person's body is 'saying.' From handshakes to posture, everything about them is telling you something. In this course, I was taught to discern whether the words they were saying to me was consistent with their body language. Were they telling me one thing with words while their body was telling me something else, or were all channels of communication working harmoniously?

As important as this is to see in someone else, it is as equally important to see it in yourself. Are you genuinely interested in your negotiatee? What's your body telling them about your interest? Are your eyes avoiding contact with theirs, your arms crossed or your feet pointing at the nearest exit?

Or, for a better connection, are you open, leaning in and mirroring their movements? Mirroring (copying their body language) is most often done non-intentionally and instinctively, especially when we're comfortable with the person we're with, or like someone. Mirrors work magic. You may mirror a person using your body language. You may also mirror a person using their own words. Repeat the last 3 words or the last 1 to 3 words of what someone has just said. We fear what's different and are drawn to what similar.

Mirroring is the art of insinuating similarity which facilitates bonding. Use mirrors to encourage the other to empathize and bond with you. Watch two people in love at a restaurant or café to see what I mean. Be aware of what your body language is projecting. Your body will communicate more than your words will so be aware of yours at all times to project the very warmest and most trustworthy of messages.

Additionally, is your body language open, friendly and inviting? Be aware of what your body is saying at all times and remain in control of it. You won't have to worry about it if you're genuinely confident, friendly and focused on your negotiatee. Your body language will convey so much to your negotiatee and will have an affect on the outcome of the negotiation.

Body language: theirs

As important as it is to be aware of your body language, it is just as important to be cognizant of theirs. I studied body language throughout my career and especially so when I was trained as a polygraph examiner.

Often referred to as a lie detector, the polygraph instrument only works when the polygraph examiner does his or her job exceptionally well, not leaving it entirely up to the science. Doing so would invite failure. The polygraph instrument is nothing without the 'lie detector' who operates the instrument in their quest to determine truth or deception, both through the use of the instrument and the examiners own tuition.

This next story is one that showcases much of what you've learned so far and it is a great example of the importance of watching your negotiatee's body language for subtle or sudden changes.

I remember a gang member being brought to my office by the Homicide Squad because they suspected that he had vital information in the killing of a rival gang member and the specific location where the body had been hidden. The homicide squad can be very persuasive in getting suspects or witnesses to "voluntarily" present themselves to take the test, and they had alerted me a few days prior that they had their sights on this particular gang member and that they had *managed* to talk him into coming to take a test. When he arrived in the company of 4 homicide investigators, I could tell immediately that he wasn't impressed or happy to be there.

Once I had led him into my polygraph examination room and identified myself to him as a police officer, I introduce myself using my first name and last name, dropped my title, extended my hand to him and invited him to call me Paul. In this case, the gang member wasn't at all receptive to receiving my hand for the shake. Despite this, I kept my hand out for a few seconds, and in a very understanding voice, I told him that I understood his discomfort.

I looked at him right in the eyes with a smile both on my lips and in my eyes. He mumbled something about hating all cops. I leaned into him as though I had a secret to tell him and I responded by telling him that I didn't particularly like most of the guys I was working with as well, because many were assholes. I told him that many of them couldn't be trusted as far as I could throw them and that I was so glad I didn't have to work out on the streets with them. And I wasn't lying. Many of them I didn't particularly like. Ok, many of them I did. But I projected sincerity, and it was by understanding the person sitting across from me, where he was coming from and how he felt about me and the cops he'd dealt with in his world that helped me reach him to begin building rapport. I put myself in his shoes and looked at things from his point of view – he didn't need another hard-nosed idiot cop barking orders and telling him what to do. He needed someone understanding, informing him that his opinion mattered and that I wasn't there to give him a hard time or make him do anything he didn't want to.

Once he saw that I was treating him differently from the detectives who brought him in, he finally looked at me. I established the purpose of our meeting – that the detectives felt he had vital information that could help them in the investigation of a homicide; and then I dropped it to re-visit later when the time was right. I watched his facial expressions, the shifts in his body language and listened attentively to each word he said. I noticed that the mention of him having vital information about the homicide made him very uneasy: he leaned so far back in his chair it could have snapped. His eyes went immediately to the floor, and I could almost hear him gulping.

I watched him carefully to assess his body language, and I was cognizant of my own body language and what I was communicating to him nonverbally through it. In this case, he entered my room with no trust in me or the police whatsoever... at first. Imagine yourself in a negotiation that went wrong, perhaps through the incompetence of another negotiator (i.e., in his case, the detectives that brought him in.) You may find yourself facing what appears to be an overwhelmingly difficult task when in fact, it's not that difficult to overcome.

As I spoke softly to the young gang member sitting across from me, I strategically chose not to discuss the purpose of his visit with me at that stage but rather asked questions about himself to get a conversation going. I wanted to start with a conversation so that rapport could be built. I looked to discover some commonalities between the two of us, something that could help with the task of getting him to relax, like me and trust me as a person. Had I jumped immediately into the discussion or the polygraph examination, I would have received nothing from him. Even if the polygraph would have registered deception in his answers, he'd exercise his right to say nothing.

Taking whatever time is necessary to establish a good rapport on our way to relationship at the beginning of the negotiation is extremely important. And it's effective. The next hour we just sat, chatted and laughed. His body language quickly went from defensive and closed (arms crossed, legs crossed, head and body turned away from me) to being open and relaxed (now facing me with no crossed arms or legs, a genuine smile and leaning in when the moment naturally called for it). Nothing was said about why he was there to see me. I didn't bring it up.

He showed me pictures of his two daughters on his mobile device, and that's what built that bridge of "know you, like you, trust you" between the two of us, because I too spoke of my own two girls; and that's what we shared in common: a love for our wonderful children. I could tell he loved both his daughters as much as I did mine, and we were enjoying our conversation. I imagine the detectives who brought him in were wondering if I was ever going to get to the *purpose* of this meeting, as they were listening in and watching us from a video room next door, but I didn't care – I knew what I was doing. I had a plan: what I have now come to create as PIER™ negotiating.

After about an hour, the young man I'd connected with looked at me and said, "So, Paul, what do you want to know?" *I didn't ask him* – he asked me. And he used my first name. I told him what we needed from him – the body site and the 'who done it.' And this is where the *discussion* began - an hour after we'd met, and after I'd established rapport. Albeit, it wasn't a long discussion - he now *wanted* to help.

He needed assurances first that his name would not be brought up in the investigation and that no one would know who had provided the police the information. I consulted with the detectives outside my polygraph suite and they gave me with their assurances and promise that his name would never be disclosed. I trusted that – it was a cop code and the use of 'reliable informant' was enough to satisfy the prosecutors and the courts.

As far as consulting with the homicide detectives for assurances? Sometimes you don't always have the answers readily available, but your job is to find out before making any promises you can't keep. One of the absolute worst things you could ever do in a negotiation is lie to the person sitting across from you.

I returned to the young man, sat down and assured him that his name would never be disclosed. He provided the information we needed quite happily and that resulted in the discovery of the body and later the arrest of another gang member. That's what I call a successful negotiation. In this case, I was negotiating for information. And I got it.

Tone and pitch

Using the right tone in your voice helps to set the mood and help determine the direction the negotiation will take. Tone is one of the many ways we communicate our message. Using a friendly, easy-going tone and leaving the business-serious one behind will help establish connection and rapport. If things get more intense or stressful in the negotiation, slow it down. Use that low, calm, downward inflected voice to show that you're in control. This is especially critical when you're negotiating something that's simply non-negotiable. It tells the other person that you've got a handle on it and know where to take the negotiation.

Among the many things I was taught and later taught in my interrogation classes was the importance of using the right tone and projection of voice, asking the right kinds of questions and using the right body language. Your body language must be consistent with your intent *and* with your words. If they're unbalanced, the person sitting across from you will detect it, and it will affect them and their subsequent decisions. Your body language, tone, and pitch of voice must always be in sync.

You must also be willing to nurture the person who is sitting across from you, much like you were nurtured in your yesteryears. Think back to when you were a child, for example. What worked best for you? Being told to do something or being spoken to with a soft, comforting and encouraging voice? And as you grew older, was it not this approach that worked best on you? Remember, what you have to say in that negotiation and how you say it is important to

your negotiatee, as much so as it is to you. And what they have to say is important to you, as much as it is for them. Not only can your words be comforting and nonaggressive, so can your body language. Never underestimate the importance of *how* you say something. I use the following example in my negotiations keynotes to drive home the importance of listening and speaking effectively in negotiations. I write the following on a whiteboard:
"I didn't do that."

Then I ask different attendees to read it out loud. At first, it all sounds the same because each participant wouldn't think to stress a particular word. Then I ask them to do something different. I ask them to choose one word in the sentence to stress.

"*I* didn't do that." When you hear the "I" being stressed, you are led to believe that the speaker didn't do it, but he or she likely knows *who* did.

"I **didn't** do that". By stressing the word "didn't", the speaker is telling you that they **didn't** do it.

"I didn't **do** that." Here, one can draw the inference that the speaker didn't "do what they've been accused of doing," but they may have been thinking of doing it, or they may have had somebody else do it.

And finally, "I didn't do **that**." Here the emphasis is on the word "that," which draws the receiver of the message to believe that the speaker did something else - something other than "that."

You can see that by stressing certain words, the receiver of the message will receive an entirely different message each time. One sentence carefully spoken can leave the receiver of the message thinking one way or another, depending on what you've stressed and how you've stressed it.

Nurturing does not show weakness or put you at any disadvantage. In fact, when you look at some of the most influential and successful people in the world, they have a soft, nonaggressive tone of voice. They effortlessly put you at ease as opposed to agitating you. And they get what they want because of their nurturing approach. Imagine John F. Kennedy in his address to the his fellow Americans, "Ask not what your country can do for you but what you can do for your country." Said in a nurturing nonaggressive way and it made an impact. Martin Luther King's speech, "I have a dream" had the same effect on the world, and it was nurturing and professional.

Don't mistake nurturing for seeming weak. I enjoyed the success of about an 80 - 85% confession rate when dealing with all types of criminals. Murderers, rapists, child molesters and robbers all responded better to a detective, me, sitting across from them who was nurturing, understanding and open to hearing their fears and *their* side of the story. The same is true with your negotiatees.

You can also imagine that as a hostage negotiator, my nurturing voice (late night radio hosts) was more likely to get me the cooperation of the hostage taker rather than using an aggressive, demanding tone - one that left them with no option but to say "No." Your tone of voice, your body language and your choice of words must all be carefully considered, executed and in sync. At first, you may have to put extra effort into making that work for you, but once you understand the importance and start becoming aware of it more consistently, it will come quite naturally to you.

Voice Projection

Hostage negotiators use one of three voices. The first is a positive/friendly voice. It's the tone of voice you're going to want to use when you first meet and greet your negotiatee. It's warm and friendly and welcomes your negotiatee to mirror that same voice and attitude (the boomerang theory). It's the voice of someone who is a good-natured and easy-going person. It's projected by the very tone that you use as well as the smile you have on your face.

Next is a slower, deeper voice. It's the voice of someone who is calm, reasonable and in control. This voice has a lower pitch to it and is most often used to slow things down and whenever there is a sense of conflict or excitement that arises during the negotiation. By deliberately lowering your voice slightly and slowing it down, it helps re-establish control and consequently, calmness. This method can be used in all your negotiations, no matter what you're negotiating for, or with whom. It's often used in conflict resolution, which I'll cover more in depth later.

The third voice, seldom used – is an aggressive voice that signals dominance to the person hearing it. It is not recommended in any of your negotiations.

Using the right 'voice' is as important as using the right body language. Be aware that people will pick up feelings from a tone of voice you use and not only your words. It will either help calm them and open them up to you, or it will do the opposite and shut them down.

Become an investigator

In many ways negotiating is much like conducting an investigation. Your job is to draw out as much information from your negotiatee as possible before you can make an informed decision; a good way of doing that is by asking questions. Asking questions is an excellent way of demonstrating that you don't have all the answers. This will not be seen as a sign of weakness. In fact, by asking questions to draw out more information from your negotiatee, you'll come across as more professional. In the mind of your negotiatee, they'll see you as a negotiator who cares enough to get all the facts.

When *you* listen carefully to a person's question, you can often discover the subtexts behind the original question asked. Subtexts are the extra information you're after - the information (or additional questions) hidden inside the original question. A question often provides a hint of what they're really after, or what they plan to ask next and needs to be answered. Your job as a good investigator is to draw out as much information from your negotiatee as you can by asking questions following their lead. You're not there solely to provide information by answering their questions. By doing that, they may get the answers they need to a point, but you will have missed an opportunity to draw much-needed information from them in order to help them make a better choice.

In business, for example, something as simple as your negotiatee asking you, "How long has your company been in business?" may mean "What I'm worried about is whether your company has enough experience and resources to handle our business." You can choose to reply to this type of question by providing them the answer they're looking for and more by also following up with a question of your own: "John, we've been in business for five years. In that five years, we've been able to accomplish xxx. Are you concerned that we may not be able to meet your needs?"

Hearing the subtext in the question can help answer their underlying concerns, not to mention that you'll come across as being professionally inquisitive - not afraid to deal with whatever their concerns may be. Far too many people are afraid of identifying a problem and simply dealing with it. By getting the jump start on this, you leave a favorable impression in your negotiatee's mind. By using this approach, you may draw out their fears so you can deal with of each them and "discuss" each point that requires exploration.

Ignoring a concern will not lead you anywhere but into a failed negotiation. Remember, you're negotiating in their world so that you can get yours taken care of as well. Be inquisitive and draw out as much information as possible. Don't be too quick to answer. For example, if your negotiatee says: "I don't like this," instead of answering, "Well we can fix it," the better response would be: "And?" (the 1-2-3 concept of repeating to draw out more information). I touched on this method earlier but it's so effective, re-visiting it here is worth the brief re-examination.

Using the word "and," for example, is an easy way to draw out more information. To repeat the above example:
Negotiatee: "I don't like this."
You: "And...?"
Negotiatee: "And I'm worried that you won't be able to deliver."
The "and" drew out the objection. It's an effective way of drawing out more information. As simple as 1-2-3. You'll know which one works best for you after you've tried them out a few times. Negotiating is not only a science, it's also an art. You develop your art by understanding what works best for you. And in order to understand it, you must practice it, repeatedly.

Clarification

As important as questions are, so is the need for clarification. Don't leave any negotiation with a possible misunderstanding. Address the issues as they arise, ask questions and follow-up by clarifying the answer or the agreement. Remember that when you're after more information, you can often get it by simply repeating the last two or three words that were said. Once you've done this, and you're quite certain that you understand all the concerns and issues, repeat it to them. Paraphrase it. Follow up with something like, "If I understand you correctly John, you're concerned about whether or not we can deliver on time each month." Or, "So, if I understand you correctly, you're concerned about the fact that we've only been in business for five years. Am I right, John?"

If this should happen to be during a moment of contractual agreement on their part, for which you have *both* agreed upon, having your negotiatee repeat the agreement as they see it, 2 or 3 times if necessary, is vitally important. Not only will they be repeating the agreement, but they will also be solidifying it into their minds for later. And if there was a misunderstanding, this is where it can, and must, be cleared up. You certainly don't want any agreements reached to be later misunderstood or misinterpreted. If that happens, negative emotions will result. When the agreement is finally committed to paper, there will be nothing left to clarify or adjust; no questions about that agreement will remain unexamined. It will be precisely what you have both agreed upon.

Hostage negotiation involves a great deal of psychology, and successful crisis negotiators are among the most skilled practical psychologists out there. Think about it: In typical hostage scenarios, lives are at immediate risk of violent death at the hands of depressed, suicidal, homicidal, delusional, drug-fueled, or cold-blooded hostage-takers and are often in the middle of a chaotic and uncontrolled workplace or family environment. Resolution of hostage crises may take hours or even days of incredibly focused and intense negotiation and require the use of virtually every type of skilled communication strategy in the crisis intervention skill box.

Time

Time is one of the negotiator's greatest tools. Hostage and crisis negotiations never adhere to a time schedule. You can imagine if we walked into a crisis negotiation with a distressed or suicidal person and said, "Okay Jack, I've only got an hour to deal with your crisis, so let's get it done quickly, shall we?" That just doesn't happen. If you're a business negotiator, imagine walking into the meeting and saying, "Carol, let's get this done fast. I've got a golf game this afternoon I just can't miss." Or in the case of a date, how well would the date go if you sat down and said, "Let's make this quick, shall we? The game's on at seven!"

How well would any of those statements go over? How likely would you be in receiving their undivided attention or their interest, for that matter? And how would you feel if someone kept glancing at their watch or cell phone as you were speaking? No, you've gotta plan to take time and focus on your negotiatee and their wants and desires. And they should do the same for you. Take whatever time your negotiation requires.

***

Giving someone your undivided attention
and taking the time each of you need to
reach a mutually-beneficial agreement
you're both happy is what you should
always strive to do.

***

If you walk into a negotiation thinking about your next appointment, your deadline or your tee-off time, or you're preoccupied about your personal circumstances, then the other person may very well pick up on this via clues from your nonverbal body language and your micro-expressions. You obviously won't be soul-listening. They'll feel rushed; and along with that, they'll feel that they're just not important enough to garner your full and undivided attention. Hence, you risk jeopardizing the deal.

Never rush a negotiation

As a negotiator, it's imperative to understand that a proper negotiation may take time. In our training as hostage and crisis negotiators, we were reminded to *slow it down* as one of the essential steps of gaining voluntary compliance.

Rushing is a common mistake many negotiators make. By rushing things, they risk jeopardizing the trust that they first set out to establish. One of the mistakes many negotiators make is that when they sense that the client is uneasy or not convinced about the deal, they tend to speed things up and repeat what they've just said; and that's a mistake. This is the very time to slow things down and address whatever concerns have crept into the negotiation that makes them feel uneasy or unsafe. When you get the sense that things are not going well in your negotiation, either by watching their body language or listening to the tone of their voices that signals to you that something is wrong, the tendency is to speed things up and to try to justify everything that you've said.

Hesitation or a snag doesn't mean the deal or opportunity is off. Failure is when we disengage, go back and try to convince our company to spend money and resources on a better proposal when you should have "just asked" when you first identified the potential objection or concern. Have the guts not to make the proposal more expensive by dealing with the concerns then and there. Find the courage to say what you're thinking but say so gently.

Your negotiatee will look for a person in control, and someone who can be depended upon; someone who is not in too much of a rush.

If they sense that you're in a rush (remember 'I have a golf game this afternoon I just can't miss?') whether conveyed that in your words or in your body language, they'll quickly lose respect in you and they'll naturally suspect something's wrong. It's only human nature to do so: their defense triggers will get them wondering why you're in such a hurry to close the deal, for example, and they'll plan to end the negotiation. We've all been there.

When somebody is rushing us to make a decision or to sign on the dotted line, we become naturally curious – and cautious. We see it in their body language as much as we hear it in their voice. We wonder why there's such an urgency to commit and why they're rushing us. Imagine yourself sitting across from a person who wants you to sign a deal right away. Are you not going to sit back in your chair and wonder why the rush for the quick close? You bet you are. You're going to wonder if you're being played and taken advantage of and what the catch is. You're going to wonder if you've missed something - something that will come back to haunt you later. And so it is with them.

Wanting something is fine but needing it has no place in negotiation. Many bad deals throughout history were signed because somebody was too much in a rush, or someone was made to feel like they had to rush a decision. Take your time and let the negotiation proceed dynamically and with purpose. Remember the process is more important to you than the close. If you're focused on the close more than you are in the process, you'll make mistakes, and you may very well lose everything.

Handshakes

*COVID19 alert – handshakes are a no-no right now. We're all hopeful they'll be alright to do in the not-too-distant future. Should they make a safe comeback…

Shaking hands in life and in business were common practice. They evolved from our ancient past. Whenever a primitive tribe would meet, they would show their hands, palms up to assure the other tribe that they were unarmed. It was a way of signaling, "I mean you no harm." In early Roman times it was fairly common practice to conceal a dagger in their sleeve for protection or an assault, and for that reason, a "lower arm grasp" evolved and became common practice when meeting another. That way they could each check for hidden daggers. That evolved into the modern handshake. The handshake is a way of projecting a message "Welcome, you can trust me. I mean you no harm."

Be cognizant of the way you shake someone else's hand. Your handshake cannot be too firm, but it cannot be too limp either. Who wants to shake hands with someone whose grip is too strong, whose grip is too weak or whose hand is too clammy? Your grip will tell your negotiatee a lot about you, and if you're nervous, you may just be sweating and shaking hands at that particular time project a message of insecurity to the one you're meeting. This may sound silly, but extensive courses are taught on how to shake hands correctly, so practice your handshake and be aware of what it says about you.

Wanting something is fine but needing it has no place in a negotiation. Many bad deals throughout history were signed because somebody was too much in a rush, or someone was made to feel like they had to rush a decision.

When I worked in the sexual assault unit, one of the detectives I worked along side of on several occasions loved to shake hands. Every day. The problem was, his handshake was a grip of death. Perhaps it was to make up for his small stature, but Ronnie, as nice as he was, delivered a painful handshake to whomever he met. More than once I had to say, "Dammit, Ronnie, ease up on the grip. Your fracturing my bones!" Nice guy, awful handshake. Don't be a Ronnie. Ronnie's handshakes may just 'kill' your deal.

Handshakes signal one of 3 things: dominance, "he or she is trying to dominate me and I don't like it"; submission, "this person is weak and lacks confidence"; or equality, "I think I can trust this person.

Customs

If you happen to be meeting with someone whose first language is not your own, try practicing a hello using a greeting in their spoken tongue. It's amazing how using a simple greeting in someone else's language can make a significant and wonderful difference. It opens the door to relationship and conveys a message that you care enough about them to greet them in their own language. And while we're on the topic of greetings with people of different nationalities, make sure that you research their customs as well.

I'm not suggesting that you research their customs in their entirety, but do research them enough so that you know what may be offensive to your negotiatee and what might be welcomed and appreciated.

Entrance and Engagement – Key points

- Never overlook the power of making your best *entrance* possible. The first few seconds of any negotiation is crucial to your overall success.

- People will decide within the first $1/10^{th}$ of a second or so whether they like you or not.

- To foster later collaboration in whatever negotiation you become involved in, try to set a constructive, positive tone from the very onset; greet the other person warmly and try to signal early on that you hope the two of you will be able to collaborate well together.

- Negotiations must involve both conversation *and* discussion as much as they must involve active/soul listening *and* asking the right questions. Negotiating and asking involves communicating with and without *purpose*.

- Ask open ended questions whenever possible to encourage more conversation and to create vision in the mind of your negotiatee.

- Never ignore what a person's body is 'saying.' From handshakes to posture, everything about them is telling you something. Watch for changes in comfort, for example. Be as equally aware of what your body is saying. Words, tone of voice and body must all be working harmoniously with one another – all three must project the same message in them and in you.

- Create a legitimate 'want' with whoever you're negotiating with, be it life or in business.

- If you're going to be dealing with someone whose customs are different than yours, familiarize yourself with their customs (as reasonably as you can) and then show it in your behavior. Maybe that translates to a warm greeting in their native language or avoiding handshakes.

Call to Action

- Now that you know the importance of first impressions, your call to action will be to make each and every one of your first impressions count from this day on. Whether you're walking into a coffee shop, nightclub, bar or meeting – walk in as though you matter significantly. Be confident, smile when the circumstances allow, shake someone's hand – do whatever the place or situation calls upon you to do to make that great impression.

P A R T 5

ARRIVING AT 'YES'

Chapter 6

PRINCIPLE NUMBER 4: RELATIONSHIP

The 'R' in PIER™ Negotiating – Relationship

At the age of 10, my daughter Aimée came to me and asked, "Dad, what's the meaning of life?" To say I was caught off guard would be an understatement. I slowly leaned back in my chair, in front of the Windows 95 computer I'd been playing *Duke Nukem*[24] at just moments earlier, dumbfounded. After what seemed like forever - when only a minute or so had passed, the only answer I could think of was a single word: "Relationships," I replied. I elaborated (as much as I could with my 10-year-old daughter) on the importance of building strong and lasting relationships, what it means to the quality of life and how it would help in every area of her life. Satisfied, she went back to watching Disney's *'Lion King'* with her younger sister Cassie as I sat back and marveled at her inquiry, forgetting that 'Duke' was about to be blasted to smithereens by aliens who had just ambushed him moments before because I had just dropped my guard. How could my 10-year-old daughter come up with such a profound question, I queried? And how did *I* come up with such a wise answer, I mused.

My answer has never changed. To this very day, I still believe that one of the most important things in life and in business -

---

[24] A video game series named for its protagonist Duke Nukem. Created originally by the company Apogee Software Ltd. Reference: https://en.wikipedia.org/wiki/Duke_Nukem

negotiations included, are strong interpersonal relationships. So much so, I've mentioned this quite a few times throughout this work. Successful negotiations are very much about establishing strong, trustworthy and lasting relationships. Only once strong interpersonal relationships are established on trust and cooperation can we manage to influence another into helping us reach our objectives while satisfying theirs.

In the previous chapter, that on Entrance and Engagement, the importance of making a first good impression and following that with positive engagement was anchored to the PIER™. I provided you with the science that people will decide within $1/10^{th}$ of a second or so whether they like you or not and they base that judgement, in part, on what your body and energetic vibrations are transmitting to them.

We are all pre-historically programmed to evaluate whether the person we meet is friend, foe or a potential partner. Watching another's body language for sudden signs of discomfort and change is a must, and listening for departures in the tone of voice they project can significantly help alert you to slow things down and address the issue/emotion that has surfaced in the negotiation. As much as it's important to be aware of you negotiatees' body language, it's as equally important to be aware of yours.

Prepare for the negotiation in advance and put forth your very best you throughout your engagement/negotiation. That was also your call to action. By doing so, you work on building the relationship, which is so vitally important in helping reach agreements. It's only once you've built your foundation and have developed a relationship that you can confidently ask for what you want. In business, that's asking for the commitment.

We will now explore the importance of the relationship in addition to how to effectively and completely handle objections, confirm benefits, ask for a commitment, sealing the deal and reassuring the negotiatee that the decision they've made was the right one to make.

This chapter may appear short in comparison to the previous chapters because each of the previous chapters have all led to establishing the all-important principle of **relationship**. Once you've arrived here by stepping confidently and capably along the PIER™, the relationship is solidly on its way to be firmly rooted. The rest and getting to 'yes' comes easy.

Relationship defined

The Merriam–Webster dictionary defines relationship as, "The way in which two or more people, groups, countries, etc., talk to, behave toward, and deal with each other." Let's examine that statement a little closer: "The way in which…" Ah, yes, the way in which we *talk to, behave toward* and *deal* with each other. How we put it all together, each step we take and the effort we put into it *will* affect the outcome. Now that you've followed the PIER™, you have an excellent chance to get what you ask for.

Successful negotiations in life and in business involve more than building relationships as I alluded to in "what this book is." Negotiations involve communication, body language, collecting and sharing information, confidence, finding solutions, trust, customer service and a range of other factors. It involves effective communication without manipulation and requires you to be completely present and in the moment, honest and exploratory, listening actively and acting with integrity for the purpose of reaching your objectives and helping them reach theirs. Once you've followed the PIER™ method of negotiating and feel ready and confident to ask for the commitment, you will have earned the right to ask. Let's examine how relationship in negotiations applies to your overall success and how and when to ask.

Friendly relationships

Everybody likes to be liked. But it should never be sole focus of your negotiation. That would be a critical mistake. Sure, you want your negotiatee to know you, like you and trust you, because once they do, the chances are greatly improved that they'll say 'yes' to your proposal. If you follow the steps you've been introduced to this far, 'liking' you will have developed naturally. Just as important as being "liked" however, is being **respected**. Respect is as vitally important.

In all life and business undertakings, your negotiatees will want to deal with those they also respect. If you negotiate with a primary focus on "win-win," you may be in for an unpleasant experience. Taking that approach may lead you to make decisions based on emotion as opposed to making sound decisions, as I warned you of earlier. You may find yourself thinking that you must salvage the deal (or friendship) at any cost, and that will accomplish very little for you in the overall outcome.

In business especially, imagine that the person sitting across from you isn't really interested in developing a personal friendship, they're interested in results. Most business negotiators you'll deal with have no desire whatsoever to become your 'buddy.' They just want the best bang and service for their buck.

Focus instead on being respected and on developing a working relationship built on trust. Otherwise, your negotiatee may play up on your misguided importance of partnerships and friendships - at your expense. Just as importantly, imagine what that could mean to your negotiatee if this relationship has become too friendship focused.

Depending on the one being negotiated with and the circumstances of the negotiation, they, in turn, may be afraid to say *no* to you. And they may agree to something *they* don't want. And you may do the same. Does that get you both an agreement of sorts at the end? Yes, it may. But not one that either one of you will be happy with in the long run and that will likely never get you another seat at the negotiation table with them again. So much for that 'friendship.' Resentment may set in, and they might just strike the deal once you're not in the room. Neither one of you wants that.

I'm not saying that friendships are not a good thing. On the contrary. They are a very good thing, but they should not be your sole focus in the negotiation. It will cause you to become too emotionally involved, and that will muddy your vision of making sound, professional decisions in the end. Ones that you can *both* live with and be happy with the outcome. Yes, in this passage I'm referring heavily to the business negotiation.

Life negotiations are obviously different. Imagine it this way: how hard is it to say no to a friend? I'm going to suggest to you that in many instances it's pretty hard. Have you ever reluctantly said yes to a friend and regretted it afterward? I bet you have. And I'm going to bet even further that you felt an ugly knot in the pit of your stomach when your friend asked you for the same favor later. If you respect and like your friend, and they respect and like you, they'll understand when you say no. That will be the glue that keeps you both together through thick and thin. Respect.

For all negotiators out there, despite what kind of negotiation you're involved in, what's more important than friendship at the end of the day is respect and effectiveness. Build the *relationship* – not the *friendship*. Being overly friendly can lead one to manipulate the other, and manipulation has no room in any successful and fair negotiation. It simply doesn't.

Most extremely successful negotiators out there are very successful business people. Some couldn't care less about friendships. But what do they have that makes them successful? They have business sense, and they have the know-how. They're successful because they don't allow their emotions to be the 'primary' focus of the negotiation. They deliver based on effectiveness and respect. And that's what makes them successful. I advocate respect and politeness with all your negotiatees, at all times. People naturally like people they respect.

Don't focus on becoming long-term friends with your negotiatee which may bring with it too much emotional baggage and which will undoubtedly include guilt. Focus rather on developing professional, friendly relationships. When that happens, and mutual respect develops, perfect. When you do your job well and focus on being respectful, trustworthy and effective, the long-term *friendly* and professional relationship will naturally develop. But that will not likely include weekend barbecues or going to a golf range. For some, it might. Cool! But for most, in business, it will include future business transactions, referrals and sealing the deal you're currently negotiating for.

When I negotiated with a hostage taker, I didn't try to be their buddy. I couldn't and wouldn't get emotionally distracted. And you could well ask, why would I want to with a hostage taker? More importantly to me and the successful outcome of the negotiation was the desire to convey respect, trustworthiness, trust, and effectiveness. That's what gets results. In the interrogation room, I built relationships and respect. I was friendly, and trust was naturally established. I didn't need to join them for a beer after work for that relationship to last. Remember how I told you that many of them would wave at me and cooperate, months later? Remember Aaron, for example? Relationships, yes. Absolutely. Friendships not always so much. It all depends on the circumstances.

Fear of hurting other people's feelings: the consequence of being *too* emotionally connected in business negotiations

Imagine your negotiatee as being a long-time friend. Now you're about to negotiate your product or service or try to make the sale. The negotiation involves money and commitment. You like your negotiatee. He or she is your friend after all. And you don't want to hurt their feelings. You're *afraid* to hurt their feelings, even if what is being proposed is not right for you. It may cost you the friendship if you do, or at the very least it will strain the friendship. So you're going to focus on not hurting their feelings to maintain the friendship, and what will cost you?

Anxiety, for one, is what it costs you – and perhaps an unsatisfactory deal. And that may take the focus away from making sound decisions that are right for each of you. That fear of not hurting the other person's feelings may cause you to focus on the end result (a so-called win-win) as opposed to the process and on focusing on what is truly important in the moment: rational, wise and result based decisions. It may prevent *you* from using the word "no" when you really want to - when you really need to. And those nagging little voices in your head will keep you hostage to thoughts like:

"This isn't right for me, but I don't want to hurt their feelings."
"How can I get out of this without hurting their feelings?"
"This isn't right for me. But I'll just say yes and live with it."

And I guarantee you that those thoughts will paralyze you from making professional, effective and rational decisions. If you're too focused on the *friendship* and not the *relationship,* you may be too afraid to make any effective decisions whatsoever. And all that time and energy will have been wasted for nothing. In a negotiation, you're not looking to make a friend. You're looking for a 'friendly relationship,' and there's a difference.

What it may do is cause your 'friend' to lose respect for you because you were unable to handle the negotiation effectively. You may leave them with no answer or certainty, and that can lead to ramifications later down the road that will jeopardize that relationship you thought you had, the one you worked at establishing by getting too emotionally attached. So instead of living with the fear of making the wrong decision or hurting somebody else's feelings, focus first on being fair, professional, trustworthy and respectful.

If you're locked into the idea of being a friend first, you're going to make mistakes and continue to make them repeatedly until you change that mentality. Until you begin to understand and appreciate **your** *value*, **your** self-worth and what **you** bring to the table, you will have no lasting success. You need a clear and focused mind on the process, and on the decisions you'll be making both for your benefit and for that of your negotiatee. Negotiations are a series of decisions and making the right decisions leads to success.

Please don't misunderstand me. I'm not saying you can't be friends. I'm simply warning you that if you are, make sure you're both completely honest with one another and discuss what may be a snag for each of you in the negotiation. In most cases, however, keep it friendly, yes, but build a relationship of likeability, trust and respect first. No need to join at the hip for life.

Handling objections

Objections are bound to happen in some negotiations but not all. Now that you have prepared, engaged and are well into building the relationship (one of friendly-ness and respect), they'll be easier to handle. They happened for me in the interrogation room as well as with my dealings with hostage takers. The important thing is never to ignore them or to speed things up and repeat what you've just said. Like 'white elephants in the room,' they must to be acknowledged, explored, understood and resolved. You do this first by acknowledging the objection.

A series of well thought out questions and/or statements helps here. For example, if your negotiatee has brought up a concern (i.e., "Yeah, but what about…"), you reply with: "I'm glad you brought that up, Suzie. Let's discuss that in detail. I want you to be completely comfortable with…", or, "I understand your concern, John. I want to examine that with you so that you'll completely understand what it involves", or "John, let's not go any further with this negotiation until we address your concerns completely." These examples are but some of the ways to show empathy and a willingness to address any of the objections that may arise in your negotiation. It's imperative that you slow things down just as you did when an emotion popped into the room.

It's important not to focus on what *you* have to say here to move it along but focus rather on what *they* have to say here. Listen soulfully after you've asked open-ended questions about the objection. "Dave, what worries you about what I just proposed?" is another example of exploring the objection from your negotiatee's point of view.

Paraphrase the objection so that you are clear about it. "So, if I understand you correctly, you're concerned that…" The use of effective pauses at this stage can be extremely helpful. You want to make sure that you understand the objection from *their point of view* as clearly as you can before going any further. Your negotiatee may be objecting to something that's impossible for anyone to deliver. You may wish to point that out softly, and honestly, by providing your negotiatee facts for why it can't be delivered and suggest alternatives to their objection. Intent at this barrier in the negotiation accounts for so much, and until you've explored the objection completely, you won't be able to proceed any further to ask for a commitment.

And once you've handled the objection that came up, you can feel confident that you've earned the right to move ahead and ask for the commitment. Return to assuming that the deal is done and use your words carefully and thoughtfully, and **just ask**.

Confirming benefits

Once you've reached a point in your negotiation where your discussions have confirmed a sincere interest for acceptance in your negotiatee's mind, then follow by first **confirming the benefits** of that interest. For example, say you've been negotiating with your child whose grades need improvement before she is accepted into a college or university of her choice, that may be something as simple as asking, "Jane, I know you have your heart set on attending _____ University, and I've mentioned that I want to help you get there. Getting in gets you so much closer to your dream of becoming a _____. Wouldn't you agree that by doing some work now to improve your grades will provide you a much better chance of getting in?" (In business you'd obviously use different terminology to confirm the benefits of what you're offering).

If the answer is "Yes," it implies your negotiatee, your child in this example, is considering the proposal/solution/offer seriously.

Confirming benefits with your negotiatee helps prepare their state of mind to later accept the proposal or solution you've worked on helping them agree to. In the case of the child in this example, that's getting her to work on her grades – immediately! If they're not ready, your negotiatee will most often object right at this stage. Don't be afraid of the "No." You haven't asked for the commitment just yet. You've merely confirmed benefit.

Should an objection arise, you'll move on to using simple methods on how to handle objections you've just been introduced to. But if it's a "Yes," you'll move directly in for the commitment. Confirming benefits is essential to any act of influence or negotiation. And that may be something as simple as asking, "I'm sure you'd agree that by doing _____ , you'll get those grades up, right?" Or, "By doing _____ (describe your plan here, involving your negotiatee, your child in this example, in the process), you'll not only get your grades up, but it will make things easier for you in the long run, right?"

In the example of your child and his or her homework, your next move will be to *transition* from simply confirming benefits to asking for a commitment from them. If the child (or your negotiatee - whomever you're dealing with) responds with a *yes*, now is the time to **ask** for the commitment.

***

Confirming benefits for your negotiatee is
an excellent way of keeping them focused
on what's in it for them. That helps you ask
for a commitment.

***

Asking for a commitment

You earn the right to ask for a commitment once you've established rapport, earned trust, respect and have established the relationship. This applies to all your life and in business negotiations. Asking for a commitment really is the easiest step - getting to that stage takes longer. Asking for a commitment was the original purpose of the negotiation after all, and now you've followed the PIER™ and have earned the right to ask. The only way you'll know whether your negotiatee is committed to making a deal - or that they're interested in one, *is* to **ask**. You may ask for change and commitment in *all* your life and business dealings with individuals you wish to influence and reach agreements with - providing you've done your due diligence by following the guideposts and principles of PIER™ negotiating.

As importantly, you must also establish a desire and/or need in them that helps them easily visualize the benefits of committing to change or committing to the agreement you're proposing. It may be your child you wish to help improve in their homework/school grades or a friend who is on the wrong path. It may be a million- dollar business deal or asking for a break in rent or a discount. The list is limitless.

Whatever circumstance you find yourself in, if you want to positively influence your negotiatee to commit to your proposal, you must follow each step you've discovered thus far to create that desire to do so within them. Your goal, your end game, is to achieve the highest level of commitment from your negotiatee. Intimidation and punishment never works - you must follow the steps of PIER™ influence for greater success - and once you've done that, it's not enough to simply get a commitment - you must also ensure that the commitments made by the individual(s) sitting across from you are also kept.

Asking for the commitment comes easy if you've followed the PIER™

If you've followed the PIER™ to this point, asking for the commitment really is quite easy. You're now ready to ask. Choose your next words carefully - your next approach is extremely important. Be direct and confident. If what you've offered as a solution is one you believe in (as it must be) and you feel confident in knowing that they're feeling good about it too, you must project that confidence in your own behavior and in your words.

There are several excellent techniques in asking for the commitment. In the aforementioned example of your child and his/her homework, you already know that you've confirmed that the solution you proposed (getting homework done/improve grades to impress the university they have their heart set on getting into) does address your child's goals. He/she told you it did. So you want to follow that up by using words that *assume* they've *already* committed, for example: "When do you want to get started?" You may also give them options: "Would you like to start off with - _____ first and _____ next?" Or, simply be direct: "I'd like you to get started now." Using these assumed commitment statements work amazingly to solidify commitments.

If this is a business deal, it's time to talk logistics. Discussing logistics helps you to completely seal the commitment that has just been made. Without this kind of follow-up, you may jeopardize the commitment that the individual has just made to you and to themselves.

Once someone has agreed to a change or to a commitment, your job is to *summarize* it and provide direction on how to make it work. Without doing that, it's possible that "fear of change" or "buyer's remorse" may kick in at the last second. Don't miss this step. There is no way for you to really know what steps your negotiatee may wish to take despite your suggestions, but you can certainly help guide them with the plan you had coming into the negotiation. Remain flexible however and *involve them* in what happens next.

Now is the time to take them from commitment to action. This will involve a calculated discussion of what happens next. It may be as simple as saying, "That's great. What would you like to start with first?" or, "Excellent. I'll help you set things up; how about we meet in a week from now to see how it's going?" In the case of a business negotiation, the contract is next. Craft it exceptionally well, and if you don't have a contract lawyer, I suggest you get one. My brother Robaire[25] is an exceptional well-established Ottawa-based contract lawyer who has guided me more than once on the importance of having a solid, bullet-proof contract, one that leaves nothing out and nothing that can be later challenged. This is where the business negotiator seals the deal.

Ah, but you're not quite done yet. In every successful hostage negotiation that I've conducted, I never omitted the important step of "reassurance." Reassuring your negotiatee that the decision that they've just made was the right one is essential and necessary step in any negotiation or act of influence, be it in business or in life. It's important for you to comfort the person who's just made a commitment to you. This may be as simple as saying, "You'll be very happy with this. I'll be here for you every step of the way." Most people who make a commitment to change often wonder if they've made the right one later on. Assure them that they have, "You're doing the right thing" is a simple statement of reassurance that goes a long way.

---

[25] http://www.kerrnadeau.com/

***
Reassuring someone they've made the right
choice by saying 'yes' to your proposal
helps put them at ease.
***

We're funny that way. You pull out your wallet to pay for a big-ticket item, and you can't help but wonder whether you've made the right decision or not. Sure, you've made that commitment, but those nagging self-sabotage hostage-taking voices in your head are at play, making you question your well thought out decision. It happens to us all. When the salesperson, in the example of the big-ticket item reassures you that you've made a great choice, it helps. Your job as the negotiator is to reassure your negotiatee that they've made the right decision too. Tell them so.

I did so with criminals who confessed. I assured them that they'd made the right decision by confessing. It reassured them. This is especially important if it's a big change or decision, a big-ticket item, and a huge commitment. We're all similar after all. We all wonder if buying into that "something," that "change," that "commitment" is the right thing for us to do. Most of us fear change. So let's help eliminate that fear in our negotiatee by using simple reassurance.

The next time they hear those "hostage-taking" voices in their heads, questioning them as to whether they've made the right decision or not, let's help change those voices of self-sabotage by replacing them with what we've provided them instead: reassurance. Don't worry; they'll hear your voice next time the voices of self-sabotage start digging at them. Your job in getting that to happen is to provide a well-worded phrase of reassurance. With a criminal confession, for example, I'd say, "The hard part is now behind you now. You've done the right thing, Sam. I'll be here to help you in whichever way I can."

Remember, the art and method of positive influence as outlined in the PIER™ principles is made up of more than just words. It's not enough to use well-thought phrases. Your body language, tone of voice and facial expressions must convey the same message. They must work in sync. My suggestion for doing this properly is to be present "in the moment." By this I mean, if you truly believe that what you've proposed is the best solution for them, let it show not only with what you've said, the spoken word, but in how you feel: your body language and tone of voice equally. They must all work harmoniously. If you feel doubtful, guess what? They'll feel it too. If you feel confident, guess what? They'll feel that too. It's unnecessary and even counterproductive to go over everything more than twice, depending on the deal and your negotiatees' needs of course.

The Apartment: A fine example of putting it all together

I'd like to finish this chapter off with a personal story to illustrate how much of what I covered throughout this book came together in a simple life negotiation. Although not all points are covered in this example, you'll appreciate how my method works and may use this very blueprint in your next apartment hunt – or a number of other asks or negotiations you're about to undertake.

Early in 2016, I was in the market for an apartment. I'd been living in a loud and bustling neighborhood in an apartment above a coffee shop. The apartment was in an older building and had character – but that's about all. As I'd come to discover, the single paned windows were so damned inefficient at keeping the harsh winter winds from whistling right through them, jacking my heating costs sky high. The 3 AM catcalls outside the building had become extremely annoying, and the endless sirens from the fire hall a block away at all hours of the night and day had lost its original appeal. It was time for a move. The lease was up, and I was no longer bound to stay.

As fate would have it, a Facebook friend I'd met through the acting community posted pictures of a lovely apartment she was vacating, asking if any of her contacts might be interested in renting it. Having moved to the big city from a country home just a couple of years earlier, I'd hoped to find an apartment in an old Victorian home someday just like the one she'd posted. Living in a big city and finding such a place at a reasonable price was next to impossible to do, especially in the *downtown* core of a bustling city. The place my Facebook friend posted just happened to be in a beautiful Victorian home and looked quite dazzling by the pictures she'd posted. What are the chances of that? It was exactly what I'd hoped to find.

I reached out to my her to make inquiries and schedule a time to see it. I met with her the next day, and the place was as beautiful, if not more so than the pictures that she'd posted. And the location was perfect. Was I dreaming? The only problem that I could see though was that this stunning apartment, complete with two spacious floors, a fireplace, a deck and two bedrooms was more than what I needed *and more expensive* than what I was prepared to pay. But I liked what I saw and asked her to put me in touch with the owner. Timing accounts for so much in everything in life, and when it comes to finding the right apartment in a big city, especially so.

I had a plan. I figured, "I'm a negotiator - there's always room to negotiate and make an offer." Why not try? Why not "just ask?" A meeting was quickly scheduled, and I met with the owner's daughter Kelly - my landlord to be *if* I struck a deal. Unnecessarily delaying this meeting for any period of time could have, and would have, cost me any chance of securing it. Move quickly when there's an opportunity to do so, otherwise, you may never even get in the door. Hesitation kills.

My friend had been paying $2500 a month which included heat, Hydro, parking, and Internet. Amazing, especially in a big city and right downtown, but too expensive for me, a single man on a fixed income. When I first met my potential landlord, I introduced myself using my first name (it applied in this case) and called her by hers; I began to establish rapport immediately. I intended to use the PIER™ – each step of it. Establishing rapport can be as simple as making that good first impression, dressing the part, greeting the other warmly using first names (mine and theirs), chatting about the weather, the neighborhood and whatever else comes to mind. A sincere compliment helps too – in this case, how wonderful the apartment was.

Establishing rapport establishes trust, and only once trust is established can you proceed to your purpose and onto the negotiation. Asking the right questions is equally important to determine what your negotiatee is thinking, what they may be looking for in the deal or transaction, and what their concerns might be. This, as you now know, is exploratory dialogue. You must ask the right questions, otherwise, you will miss out on some vital information that will help you move forward with all the available facts to reach a deal. In this instance, by asking a few thoughtful questions, I was able to gather some extremely valuable information.

It turns out that my 'friend' had moved into the apartment with one other young woman. That had been their original arrangement, albeit it was never added to the tenant contract (an example of the importance of having a solid contract in place.) However, over the course of the year, just a month or so into the lease, she invited three other girls to move in with them. The place was certainly large enough to accommodate everybody, but it was not part of their original agreement. It blindsided the owner who had to incur additional expenses for heat, hydro and water, not to mention the traffic coming in and out of the apartment.

Kelly ran a small business on the first floor, and the entrance and exits to the apartment above were made passing the office by each time. I could tell in Kelly's voice and in her body language that this was a concern and sore point her parents (the owners) and she had in renting to someone else (objection identification). This I knew was a huge objection – one I absolutely needed to address. I casually assured Kelly that I wouldn't do that if I were to move in and that anyone who joined me would first have to be approved by her. I could sense that by addressing this "white elephant in the room" – her concerns and that of her father (who owned the house), she was much more at ease. A smile came to her face, and I could tell immediately by her body language that she was comforted by the assurance I had just given her.

Once rapport had been established (the engagement, which leads to the relationship) and after addressing her objection, I had a thorough look around while still building rapport and making conversation and decided to make my offer. One might think that apartment rental prices are all fixed and there's no room for negotiating. But that simply isn't so, especially if the rental is privately owned, and it's not so with a multitude of other opportunities as well. I thought to myself, "I like this place. Why not ask if there's room for price negotiation?"

I had by now built the foundation on which move forward. In a short period of time, I had earned the right to ask. I knew it would be mutually beneficial for both of us if I were to become the new tenant. I paused for a moment, looked at my prospective landlord and provided her with a little extra incentive and another reason to say 'yes.' I continued, "I really like this place Kelly. It's exactly what I've been looking for. I know you don't know me just yet, but I can assure you that when I move in[26], I'll take good care of your place – as though it were my very own, and I'll be an ideal tenant for you and your parents. I can provide you with whatever references you need. And I can move in almost immediately." I paused for a moment… (pauses are often very powerful in negotiations before moving further) and continued, "But I'm afraid the price is a little bit too high for me. Now I don't know if there's any room for negotiation here, but I'm hoping there is. Let me ask you, do you think your dad would be prepared to accept $2000 a month?" *Without* hesitation, the answer was, "I think that's possible. Let me ask and get back to you within a day." I smiled at her, shook her hand and added, "If he agrees, we've got a deal."

That night I received an email from Kelly informing me that her father had accepted my offer. The contract was attached. Now when you do the math, a savings of $500 a month over a year is $6000. Not bad for 'just asking' (by deploying the PIER™), right? Use this approach in your next negotiation and you may very well save yourself a ton of money, which will more than cover the cost of this book! This applies to any of your life or business negotiations). Just ask – you'd be surprised what you might get. As an important follow-up, I replied to Kelly's email assuring her and her father that they had made the right decision and how I looked forward to living there.

---

[26] The choice of words in this instance provided an assumption in her mind that I was already her tenant

Examining the 'Apartment' negotiation: simple lessons on effectiveness

Let's dissect this simple, yet important transaction further. Imagine it as a blueprint for your next negotiation. No, I wasn't negotiating for a multimillion-dollar business deal or to save a life, but an opportunity arose to negotiate in a day-to-day life transaction which saved me $6000 a year because it was handled correctly. The principles of negotiation apply to day-to-day negotiations as much as they do to million-dollar business negotiations. You know this now.

Knowing what I could afford for rent before I visited was crucial. I wouldn't budge from what I'd decided was the most I could afford, no matter how appealing the apartment was. After all, had I not secured this one, I'd keep looking for the next and apply the same PIER™ principles in that negotiation. I knew my bottom line. I was ready to walk away if the answer would have been 'no' and if there was no room to negotiate. The same is true in any business or life negotiation. Know what you're prepared to give and know what you're prepared not to. Walking away when no deal can be reached and/or no further negotiation can take place is what you must be prepared to do. By doing so, you acquire an immediate 'win' for yourself.

The moment I arrived, I began establishing rapport with her by projecting positive body language, along with a good handshake, a sincere smile, a warm hello and using our first names to personalize our meeting. I dressed appropriately for the meeting – a hint of business attire, wanting to add to that good first impression - as though I was meeting someone for a first date. Yes, you read that correctly. Wouldn't you want to dress your best to meet a potential partner for the first time? I hope you answered 'yes' to that. The same holds true in business and all life negotiations. Dress to impress. Dress for the occasion, whatever that may be.

Rapport building began the moment I walked in and included a simple conversation (i.e. how nice the neighborhood was, queries about her small business and so on) which eventually led to the discussion – the negotiation – and the right to ask when the timing was right. By the time I mentioned what I could afford, I'd established a positive connection with Kelly, providing me the *right* to ask for the discount. Now keep in mind that every negotiation will be different. Negotiations are dynamic and unique - some take longer than others to reach the point of asking.

When we dissect this simple negotiation even further, understanding human nature applies in this situation as much as it does to any other negotiation you'll enter into. What do landlords want? Landlords want someone they can rely on - someone who pays on time and will take good care of their place. Planning your answers before you meet with your client or prospect is vitally important to any negotiation. Now don't confuse this with having a 'script.' It's not. A script must be followed to the letter whereas planning answers for what might be asked only makes sense. A script, as you now understand, does not allow for deviation from it, whereas having a plan on what to say allows you the flexibility to go with the flow or create your own opportunities to inject what it is you'd like to emphasize.

In your business negotiations, for example, you'll be asking what your client wants and hopes to get from the deal. Isn't that what I did in this negotiation? You'll be asking what they expect of you and/or from your service. For your customers in retail, you'll be asking what they expect over and above the product you're offering. Are they looking for an extended warranty? If not, asking the right kinds in a calculated friendly fashion will get them thinking about extra warranties. And when you don't know what their needs or desires are, you'll be asking exploratory questions to get that information. In this case, I'd asked exploratory questions to get a sense of what my landlord(s) were looking for, and I'd done my homework: I'd considered their needs from their point of view and had my answers prepared – not by script, but by emotion and flow. I was prepared, my intention was not solely self-focused, my entrance and engagement was deliberate, and I asked only after each step of the PIER™ had been successfully applied.

The Apartment: An in-depth summary

- Never pass on an opportunity to ask. In this scenario, I liked what I saw – despite the obvious: it was more than I could afford. "I'm a negotiator, there's always room to make an offer" has always been my approach since creating the PIER™, and once you commit the PIER™ Principles of negotiating to memory, so must you. Why not try? Why not "just ask?" The worst they can say is "no."

- In a scenario like this one, time is of the utmost importance. To delay would have surely resulted in the loss of this great opportunity. An apartment like that one does not last long on the market in the busy city. Same is true in life and in business negotiations. Hesitation could cost you the deal. Considering the PIER™, the P in PIER™ is planning. Plan to make your move quickly. Plan on what you'll say, how you'll say it and move forward without hesitation.

- Introducing yourself by using your first and last name and then asking the other to call you by your first name is extremely important. It helps create familiarity, and people will want to deal with someone they know, like and trust. Do so with them. I didn't feel the need to introduce myself by using my last name in this instance, however. I wanted to keep it intimate, and I knew it would be a very short meeting. Don't use their last name or their title whenever possible. That is, providing you are not disrespectful, speaking to Queen, for example. But the rule of thumb is simple: using the person's first name brings a level of comfort to the engagement. It creates a sense of familiarity.

- Establishing rapport establishes trust, and only once trust and respect are established can you proceed with the negotiation. Asking the right kinds of questions (the exploratory phase) is equally important to get to know what the other individual is thinking, what they may be looking for in the deal or negotiation and what their concerns may be. Asking something as simple as, "What would you be looking for in your ideal tenant?" will go a long way in providing you with some valuable information. Listen carefully to the answer to see if you fit their ideal image of a tenant. If you do not, remember guidepost number one, no manipulation (or lying) and end the negotiation in a friendly and honest fashion. In the exploratory questions phase, you might also want to ask, "What was it about the last tenant that didn't work out for you?" Again, an opportunity to gather some important intelligence to see if you're the right fit and to show them you're interested in their needs.

- Watch body language: yours and theirs. Listen for changes in their tone of voice, those subtle nuances that project emotion. This will help you formulate your next questions or in making a statement such as, "I sense you didn't get along with the former tenant, would I be right?" Should the answer be 'yes,' follow it up with, "What was it about them or their behavior that didn't work out?" Keep the conversation casual, friendly and inquisitive – as though you were talking to a someone you knew well and not as though you were a hard-nosed detective looking for answers. Most of us are guilty of not asking enough questions and of not gathering enough vital information.

- After having gathered important information and finding yourself in the position to move forward to ask for a commitment or consideration, assure your negotiatee (in this case, your prospective landlord) that you *are* the right fit for them and that they are making the right choice. They need assurances that the decision that they're about to make is the right one. Tell them why the deal would be a good one for them. This is the prelude to asking for the commitment. If you've followed the steps on the PIER™, you've earned the right to ask at this point.

- Be honest about price. In this case, the apartment was too expensive for me. After building a rapport, having the right intent, making a good impression, determining what didn't go well between the landlords and their former tenant and providing them with reasons why I would be the right fit, I stated the obvious. I told Kelly that I liked the apartment, but it was too expensive for me. I asked for consideration, but with something to offer in return: "I'll be a responsible and good tenant. I'll take care of your place as though it were mine". I "just asked" … But notice I asked once the foundation and value had been established.

- Take risks, just ask, and in this case, you can see that it paid off extremely well for me financially, and it also worked out for Kelly. I was true to my word; I was a good tenant. We were both happy with the way our agreement turned out.

- Finally, reassure them that they **have made** the right decision and that it will work out wonderfully. You may do this at the end of the negotiation once it's been sealed, by phone and even by email later. People feel better being assured they've made the right decision.

As we examine relationship-building a bit further, I'd like to add the following. Perhaps seeing how committing to your company as you would to your family can not only benefit you work-wise, it can also help you feel fulfilled will tie a few things in.

Why so many workers die inside, never reaching fulfilment or potential. Family values in the workplace

What I'm about to share with you could make the difference between your success as a CEO, business owner, mentor or employee. Yes, business related but everybody will benefit from the following information. Trust me.

Have you ever wondered what makes some businesses and individuals so outstanding and successful in their fields, whereas other businesses and individuals either fail in the market place or, as the individual employees, fail their organizations and themselves so badly, their lack of enthusiasm and commitment ultimately contributes, in part, to the demise of their very organization? Of course you haven't. *Unless* you're a CEO, or it's your job to evaluate what's going right and what's going wrong within your organization.

But you should, to a degree, because if you belong to an organization, you also belong to a family, and as such, you have a responsibility to your family and to yourself to be the very best you can be to help your family succeed. That's the paradigm shift I want you to make today: see your role in your organization as being the role of a family member: either a parent, big sister/brother, mentor or learner. I'll call this piece, "Family values."

A barrel of rotten apples

By now you why I joined the police service. I couldn't wait, as a child, to arrest the monster who lived in my father. And you also know that I never got that chance but at the age of 21, true to my word and my passion for helping others, I joined the police department.

There had been eye hiring freeze and when I was recruited, I was among 10 or so other new constables and we were all assigned different platoons to work on. I happened to get placed on a platoon of senior officers, many of whom were "career constables." Career constables are constables who have either chosen to remain uniformed patrolmen their entire careers or never got promoted for whatever reason. After working a very short period of time with my new platoon of senior cops, I think I know why these guys never made it beyond the uniform. Just about every one of those officers on that platoon were so bitter, they spent most of the time complaining about how the police department had done them wrong. I had to sit eight hours a day or night beside one of these bitter cops listening to their "poor me" monologues, day after day, night after night, and it affected me. It affected me so much so that I considered quitting the police department in pursuing an acting career. I had been placed in a barrel of rotten apples and I was becoming rotten myself.

So why tell you this story? What could this story possibly do with your organization or with you as an individual?

What is often lacking in the workplace these days is the spirit of generosity and the sense that an organization is a *family*. One of the best ways to succeed in any business is to treat the business and every individual within the organization like family; to support each other, work with each other, respect each other and root for each other. To be as generous with each other as we would to a family member.

It's about having the spirit of helping one another out, no matter what, as opposed to making it all about "me." 90% of the workforce these days are unfulfilled because they take care about themselves only, and work should be about fulfilment, to oneself, the organization, the customer and all who come to it: partners, clients, whomever. When we join an organization, we should join because we believe in the organization and not solely in the paycheck. When leaders accept new employees into their family, it should not be because they've got the better resume. It should be because they value the same principles the organization does and they have that spirit of family commitment.

The human race is social and our survival depends on forming cultures and communities. The company you work for should be a group of people with common values and beliefs. When we surround ourselves with people who share our common values and beliefs, trust emerges. We need trust to survive. It's a feeling, and not something we can see, but we all need it to feel secure and to survive. With it, we are more likely to take risks, experiment, explore, grow, and so forth, with the confidence that those who trust us will always have our backs.

Organizations should say and do what they *believe in*, what they stand for and not solely what they think might please the customer. Imagine changing yourself to please another – are you being true to your spirit? "Hey, how do you want me to dress, to speak, to behave so you'll like me?" I'm sure many of us do that, especially if we long to be accepted and liked but it goes against our very natures. Those who like us for who we are will reply, "No, you don't have to change yourself for me. I like you because of who you are. Be you. That's what I love." Do that in your organization, be you, give your very best of you, and you will attract those who are looking for that. You can't lie or try to please everybody.

If *you* joined your organization because you believed in what it stood for, then you joined because the organization and its principles aligned with your own and that's the first step to success. It was the right thing to do. By doing that, you cannot neglect your tribal and family responsibility to do the very best you possibly can to help your family succeed. It's not like once you're adopted, you drop all the nice-person attitude and turn into an unlikeable, unproductive self-serving 'it's all about me' person. No, you made a commitment to be a part of the family, and along with that commitment comes responsibility, generosity and, yes, wonderful fulfilment so desperately needed in the work we do and our personal lives. With it, you'll be happier, more energetic and more at peace with the world. With it, you'll be contributing to the world around you and not just taking, only to feel unsatisfied in the end.

Show up and feel like a part of something bigger than yourself. Your role is to put what your family believes into words, pictures and results for your customers and for your fellow employees and family members. The more you can give of yourself, the more you trust each other, the more you work in harmony together, and that's when great things happen. Nobody gets left behind, and trust is, after all, what families need to survive and prosper.

Let's move on and talk about management and leadership for a moment. The responsibility of management is to help you realize you're capable of doing so much more than you can. The power of those who teach us confidence is that we'll remember their names for the rest of our lives.

The power in helping others find their own strengths is what management should be doing, that, and being the representative and head of the family. On the flipside of that coin, it's what you should be doing for each other. I started this brief section out by talking about bitter policemen who put themselves first and who felt so unfulfilled day after day after day. What kind of work life was that? It was great sorrow that led simply to a paycheck, and eventually to being remembered – by name - as bitter, sad cops. It undoubtedly seeped into their personal lives as well. How could it not? As much as we can remember those who have supported us and helped us throughout the years, we can also remember those who did not. I could name a few names. I'm sure you can too.

If you have someone who reports to you, your responsibility is not to have them meet deadlines. Your responsibility is not to have them do as you say. Your responsibility is to make sure that they understand their own strengths, their own values and that they know that they're way more talented than they think they are, and the only way they'll learn that is if you put them in situations in which they can fail. Your job will be to hold them, mentor them, support them, encourage them and pick them up when they fall. Your job will be to give them the talent, skills and education they need to meet their family's needs, and when and if they fall, your job will be to encourage them to get back up. Your job will be to help them back up until they can figure it out themselves. That's called building confidence and independence in the other. It's giving them the wings they need to make it on their own.

It's your responsibility to help them find their confidence, meet their deadlines and do their very best, and by doing this, you will be fulfilling part of your role as family member and contributing to your family's success. The amazing thing is that once they find it, they'll help others find theirs, and this is what builds trust and support among family members helping you all achieve your desired results.

As much as this is a management and leadership/mentor responsibility, it is also the responsibility of each and every worker who is part of that family and organization to do their very best, and by doing so, we feel fulfilled. We feel good and accomplished. We feel part of something big. When we are *unfulfilled*, we do not produce. The people you work with should care about you as much as you care about them. I'm an advocate of the simple principle that what we give to others we receive in kind. Give and you shall receive. It's the simple theory of reciprocation - the little things you do for others inspires others to do the little things for someone else. Isn't that what an organization should be all about? Isn't that what a family should be all about? Supporting each other and helping each other? But here's a word of caution for those who don't believe in being part of the family. Groups will ostracize those who don't join in until they come around. How do you create brothers and sisters out of strangers? Here's something to think about:

In the military, *nobody* gets left behind. Everyone supports each other and that builds trust among the tribe. When you get the environment right, you get the right results. Companies don't do business with companies and that's where so many companies fail. *People* do business with *people*. Workers should work with brothers and sisters, otherwise they work for themselves and risk feeling unfulfilled. When you give selflessly to your tribe and make them feel safe, you're contributing to the overall success of the family. Your company should be a family. As a good parent or a good sibling, you don't point out your family members failures. You point out their strengths. You give them undying love.

The "I -me -my" attitude must be replaced with "we," "our," and "us." Junior members just need to be good at their jobs. But leaders have to take care of those **in** their charge. Great leaders are not responsible for the results - they're responsible for the people who are responsible *for* the results. Great employees on the other hand are responsible for being great employees.

Let's take a look at the meaning of generosity before I move on. This all relates nicely to asking and negotiating – it's about attitude and commitment.

Generosity helps you get what you want

What is generosity? Generosity is doing something for someone else without ever expecting anything in return. We are part of a family when we join an organization for the right reasons. And that's the attitude we should bring to work with us every day. In fact, don't go to work. Go to produce. Go to experience. Go to create. Go to support. Go to be a part of the family. Go to grow. Go to feel fulfilled. It's amazing that once we start to take this attitude to work how much better our spirits will be as individuals. To feel fulfilled at work is when you do something for someone else. We all need this feeling to survive.

Now let me step aside here and say that this is somewhat comparable to sex. Sex was designed by mother nature to feel good, so we'll do it more often to procreate, right? It's amazing to think that when we do something to support another human being, to lift another human being, to improve their circumstances and so forth, it generates the same feel-good endorphins within ourselves.

Work in providing services to others should be about the client and not about the organization. 100% of customers are people. 100% of clients are people. Making it all about them and not about you is what creates success. And when you work with family members, you're working with people that matter to you. They share your values and are part of your tribe. For that very reason, you should be making it about them and putting 100% of yourself into helping them meet *their* goals and *their* expectations. Doing that will naturally improve your position and worth at the workplace as well as your personal lives. Your intent should be to serve. Imagine your fellow worker. Who's in the room? What do they want and what do they need? The feeling of fulfillment comes from helping others. When you don't pull your own weight at work or anywhere else in life, you're not only letting the other person down, you're letting yourself down and consequently you'll feel unfulfilled in that relationship. And the amazing thing is that when we do good for others it inspires others to do good for others. Do more with what you have.

Is this difficult to do? No. Imagine it like exercise. It's like working out. Your body builds strong when you work out consistently. If you only go in one day a week or every once in a while, to work out, you'll see no results. If you don't work out hard, you'll see no results. Strength and body results, as a result of hard work and consistency in the more you do it, the easier it becomes and the more satisfying it becomes. That's what brings about results. But balance it all – even family members need rest as does the body, mind and spirit. If you don't, you could end up self-sabotaging yourself.

Relationship – Key Points

- Over and above being "liked," in business negotiations especially, is being respected. Don't focus on becoming your negotiatee's best 'friend'; in the life/business negotiation, if you've followed the steps of preparation, intent, entrance, and engagement, they'll like you as a natural progression to your interactions, but more importantly, they'll respect and trust you and that creates the all-important 'relationship'.

- Handle whatever objections or concerns that pop up immediately. Ignoring them is like ignoring the white elephants I warned you of earlier. Fact is, they are white elephants which must never be ignored. Otherwise, they'll stay, and they'll crush you and any chance of sealing the deal, whether it be in life or business negotiations. Never ignore them: Acknowledge them, address them and satisfy them; they'll move on.

- Should you encounter an objection, slow things down and deal with it thoroughly before moving on. "I'm glad you told me that Peter. Let's examine that concern completely before moving any further. I want you to be completely comfortable with this." Or, "I understand. We're not going to take another step until…"

- You earn the right to ask for an agreement or a commitment only after you've earned your negotiatee's trust, established rapport and have established a good relationship. That and once you've created value in what you offer, of course. Asking for the agreement is one of the easier steps providing you've created the foundation on which to ask by following the guideposts and principles of PIER™.

- When you feel that your discussion (the negotiation) is going well and that your negotiatee sees and appreciates the value in what you're offering, confirm the benefits to them. Ask one answer questions such as, "Wouldn't you agree that by…." Or "I'm sure you'd agree…., right?"

- If your negotiatee confirms the benefit you've outlined, move on with a gentle approach of assuming they've already agreed and the 'deal' has been done. "I'm glad we can move forward, Jessica. When would you like to begin?"

- Reassure your negotiatee that they have made the right decision if 'yes' is what you get. "You've done the right thing. You're going to love…."

- Keep your word.

Call to Action

- This call to action is not a hard one. In all your life and in business negotiations, from this day forward, never be afraid to ask for the commitment or the agreement after you've built the foundation on which to ask. The more you become familiar with the PIER™ method, the easier it will become. Trust me. We've journeyed long enough now for *you* to reach this agreement with *me*.

Conclusion

You're here. You've crossed the PIER™ and now you're ready to become a badass negotiator! Congratulations. I told you it wouldn't be hard. Let me cover just a trickle of what I've covered and then, you're well on your way. Make yourself proud and get that job, that deal, that girl, that guy, that discount, that whatever! Just go out and ask, dammit.

The successful negotiator and proficient asker, that's now you, is one who follows the strategic plan as outlined in PIER™ negotiating. Successful negotiating requires time and practice to develop and refine. Don't limit your negotiation skills to simply business negotiations or sales – there are so many exciting and profitable opportunities to negotiate in life as well, as you've discovered throughout this book. Life and relationship negotiation opportunities are all around you.

Negotiation is, after all, simply a quest for reaching agreements and we do that every day, even if with our own selves. Focus on your negotiatee's needs and wants first, and yours will be taken care of naturally as you positively influence their outcomes using the principles and guideposts of PIER™ negotiating. Much of your success will depend on how well you can build and then improve your relationships. Never ask without first building a foundation on which to ask. But **DO ASK**.

Success comes to those who work for it. Success comes by first working on yourself; by un-hostaging yourself and negotiating influentially with yourself up first before negotiating with others. Success for you will be largely dependent on how much effort you want to put into achieving it. I've provided you with a number of time-tested techniques and observations from not only myself, but other exceptional professionals to help you achieve your very best. I've provided you with a simple formula to follow, and I encourage you to remember the acronym PIER™ and what it stands for.

By now, through my many repetitive uses of it, you won't forget! The instructor in me has prepared you for the tests: your life and business tests, that is. Using the PIER™ negotiating principles will bring you many successes. As you've undoubtedly gathered, I'm not a hard-nosed negotiator. I believe in being fair and adaptable but also in going after what I want. I recommend you follow suit. The ability to reach your personal and professional goals in negotiating lies within you and whatever effort you choose to put into it.

I warned you from the onset of this book that I'd be repeating several key concepts throughout this work, and I've been true to my word. I trust that these concepts are firmly rooted in your memory by now.

I wish you every success in every one of your negotiations, be it in life or in business. Should you wish to discuss my approach further or have me keynote speak at one of your events in person, you can visit my website at www.jpaulnadeau.com

Remember: **Just ask**

About the Author

Former police detective, hostage negotiator and international peacekeeper J. Paul Nadeau spent more than 30 years working with victims of crime and perpetrators and learning from top experts in abuse situations, murder investigations, hostage takings, terrorist attacks and human behavior in general. Over the course of his career, Paul talked hostage takers into giving themselves up and murderers into admitting to their crimes. And because of his extensive training and his unique approach to connecting with people of all walks of life and under every circumstance, his life was *saved* by a terrorist during a terrorist attack in the Middle East. Paul understands the importance of connecting to others, without judgement, prejudice or fear so that we can each contribute to helping the world become a better and safer place. He reflects this compassion in each of the books he writes, each seminar he runs, each life-coach motivational session he has and in each of his global keynotes.

As accomplished as Paul's career has been – and continues to be, his life has been equally influenced by events in his youth that were beyond his control. As a survivor of severe physical and emotional abuse by an alcoholic father, he experienced firsthand the loss of hope and destructive internal dialogue that can immobilize a person as effectively as any prison. Suffering from low self-esteem, anxiety and depression at an early age, Paul experienced a moment in grade 7 that turned his life around and led him to confidently take control of his life. He credits that moment for providing him the personal power to achieve many successes, both personally and professionally. He became the policeman he promised himself he'd become to arrest men like his father, and he has made it his life's mission to guide others through the thoughts and experiences in their lives that hold them hostage, just as his thoughts had once done to him. He now speaks to thousands of people-in large audiences and one on one about what they can do not only to overcome their fears and challenges, but also to confidently step forward into a new, happier and more fulfilled life.

Acknowledgments

I would first like to thank my wonderful and patient editorial director Jim Gifford for his guidance and direction and also for having picked up my first self-published book and turning it into a HarperCollins published work. To all the great staff at HarperCollins Canada: my heartfelt thanks. I would also like to thank my brother Robaire Nadeau for his sage advice and constant support with both my books. Thanks to Farah Bhanji for sage advice and support. Additionally, I could never have written a book on negotiations and interrogation had it not been for the Regional Municipality of Durham, more specifically, the Durham Regional Police Service who hired me as a police constable back in 1978 and provided me with so many excellent opportunities to work in a number of exciting and diverse fields of expertise. To those who hired me and to the many supervisors and leaders of the DRPS who helped my career along, thank you. To the United Nations who provided me with an opportunity to serve in Jordan in 2005 during the Iraqi war, thank you. And to all my readers and supporters: Thank You.

Bibliography

Suggested readings:

Mahan Khalsa/Randy Illig: "Let's Get Real or Let's Not Play"© 1999, 2008 Penguin Books Ltd. FranklinCovey Co.;

Jim Camp: "Start with No" © 2002 Random House, Crown Publishing Group;

Chris Voss: "Never Split the Difference "©2016 HarperCollins Publishing;

Rob Jolles: "How to Change Minds"©2013 Berrett-Koehler Publishers Inc.

J. Paul Nadeau: "Take Control of Your Life"©, 2018 HarperCollins Canada

Made in the USA
Middletown, DE
15 January 2022

58691658R00166